H.M.D.

WE LuvE You!

Old TIME Cooking For
You to get Better & Feel Fabubus.

Love You Rick & Nick

Southern Living
farmers market cookbook
a fresh look at local flavor

Southern Living

farmers market cookbook

a fresh look at local flavor

Oxmoor House

ISBN-13: 978-0-8487-3307-0
ISBN-10: 0-8487-3307-X
Library of Congress Control Number: 2009925698

Printed in the United States of America
First Printing 2010

Oxmoor House, Inc.
VP, Publishing Director: Jim Childs
Editorial Director: Susan Payne Dobbs
Brand Manager: Daniel Fagan
Managing Editor: L. Amanda Owens

FARMERS MARKET COOKBOOK
Senior Editor: Rebecca Brennan
Project Editor: Vanessa Lynn Rusch
Senior Designer: Melissa Clark
Director, Test Kitchens: Elizabeth Tyler Austin
Assistant Director, Test Kitchens: Julie Christopher
Test Kitchens Professionals: Allison E. Cox, Julie Gunter, Kathleen Royal Phillips,
    Catherine Crowell Steele, Ashley T. Strickland
Photography Director: Jim Bathie
Senior Photographers: Ralph Anderson, Van Chaplin, Gary Clark,
    Jennifer Davick, Art Meripol, Charles Walton IV
Photographers: Robbie Caponetto, Laurey W. Glenn, Beth Dreiling Hontzas
Senior Photo Stylists: Kay E. Clarke, Buffy Hargett
Associate Photo Stylist: Katherine Eckert Coyne
Production Manager: Theresa Beste-Farley

Contributors
Composer: Carol Damsky
Copy Editor: Rhonda Richards
Indexer: Mary Ann Laurens
Interns: Hannah Bunning, Georgia Dodge, Allison Sperando, Christine Taylor

To order additional publications, call 1-800-765-6400.

For more books to enrich your life, visit oxmoorhouse.com
To search, savor, and share thousands of recipes, visit myrecipes.com

contents

foreword

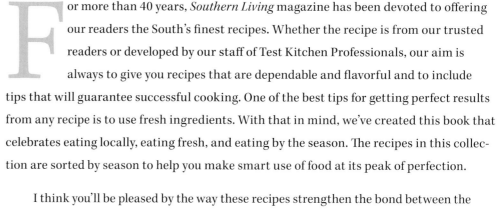

For more than 40 years, *Southern Living* magazine has been devoted to offering our readers the South's finest recipes. Whether the recipe is from our trusted readers or developed by our staff of Test Kitchen Professionals, our aim is always to give you recipes that are dependable and flavorful and to include tips that will guarantee successful cooking. One of the best tips for getting perfect results from any recipe is to use fresh ingredients. With that in mind, we've created this book that celebrates eating locally, eating fresh, and eating by the season. The recipes in this collection are sorted by season to help you make smart use of food at its peak of perfection.

I think you'll be pleased by the way these recipes strengthen the bond between the home cook and the local farmer, while fostering the joy of cooking. With dozens of Southern farmers market images included in the book, you'll feel the energizing vibe of strolling among vendors' stalls at the market, selecting fruits and vegetables from abundant garden-fresh offerings. You'll delight in the knowledge that you're preparing vibrantly tasty and healthful dishes with the freshest, most nutritious ingredients.

As you browse through the pages of this book, be sure to look for helpful advice on ingredient and recipe preparation offered in special Tips From Our Kitchen and Tips From the Farm boxes. For specifics on selecting and storing fresh produce and herbs, check out the Fresh Produce & Herb Primer on page 264. And don't miss the Farmers Market Finds chapter starting on page 278. It's filled with listings of dozens of farmers markets throughout the South, making it easy for you to locate markets in your area as well as some you may want to visit on your next vacation.

We're passionate in our desire to provide you with recipes and cooking advice that fit your healthful lifestyle. Thanks for inviting us into your home.

Sincerely,

Scott Jones
Executive Editor

the farmers market experience

Gather your family or a few good friends, and take a Saturday morning stroll around the local farmers market. In this community environment, you can savor the season's bounty of freshly picked fruits and vegetables in an array of colors and flavors and connect with friends along the way. In addition to peak produce, many markets offer flowers by the bunch, handmade crafts, and live local entertainment. You'll feel good knowing that you've selected fresh ingredients from a local vendor that will make your food taste even better.

The farmers market experience is one of simple goodness where produce, meat, and dairy farmers offer their wares straight from their lands to their customers' hands. Whether set up as roadside stops with pickup trucks loaded with that week's pick from the farm or freestanding, open-air markets offering a variety of locally grown seasonal bounty, farmers markets can be found almost anywhere across the U.S. and Canada.

Any given weekend throughout the year, these pop-up local events transform normally deserted ghost town settings into bustling centers of commerce. Men, women, and children—the young and the old alike—can be found interacting with the produce of their choice; after all, the farmers market is a hands-on experience where sight, smell, feel, and taste provide for the best selection in quality.

Welcome to the Market

Farmers markets roots in American history can be traced back to the early 1930s, when the economy experienced the Great Depression. At a time when fresh produce was not always readily available in stores and many farmers were struggling to make a living, the idea of going straight to the individual became the saving grace of these producers across the nation.

Since then, this direct relationship between farmers and their consumers has not only increased farmers' bounty of sales, but it has also highlighted and developed an American interest in organically, locally, and seasonally grown eating trends; a healthful and delicious win-win situation for all.

However, farmers markets are not solely about the produce or the price. An equally important aspect of these markets is the social setting they create. At times many of these markets operate as a mini county fair with live music, fun and games for the kids, and even small eateries offering fresh baked goods, beverages, and hot meals. Many people come together in groups to enjoy their shopping experiences in a way that can be likened to going to the mall to shop, eat, and enjoy the atmosphere. This newfound setting is one that is strengthening economic, social, and health-oriented interactions between producers and consumers season by season. So welcome to the farmers market. We're glad you came.

why buy local?

Cost: There's much to be said about the benefits of buying locally when it comes to pricing. Supporting your local farmer in turn supports your local economy. When buying produce, meats, and dairy locally, these products can be offered at lower costs simply due to the lower cost in production and transportation. Produce that must travel long distances from the grower to the seller tends to be more expensive and uses more energy to transport. By removing the opportunity for higher markups due to the exchange of products among many hands, both farmers and consumers reap the benefits of locally produced, locally sold, and locally bought farm-fresh foods.

Taste: When foods are produced locally, they are also produced seasonally. And all foods, no matter where they're from, taste better when eaten in their peak season. There's simply no better time to eat a strawberry than in the summer, plain and simple. The same holds true for all produce made available when it is grown within the timeline of its natural production. Think about it: When was the last time a tomato tasted delicious in the dead of winter?

Variety: Locally and seasonally produced fruits and vegetables also provide diversity across the seasons. This in turn allows for a versatile diet. Research has proven a healthy body should intake a daily variety of assorted produce in order to reap the maximum benefits of fruits and vegetables, as they each provide different nutrients needed to maintain a healthful lifestyle.

shopping at the market

Go early: The best produce is often found right when the market opens. Avoid choosing from picked-over produce by arriving at your local market as early as possible.

Go often: Buy only as much as you will use within a few days, and store produce (except tomatoes) in the refrigerator or in a cool, dark place. Flavor and nutrients diminish quickly.

No list needed: When visiting your local farmers market, be prepared to keep an open mind. While you might be looking for something in particular, odds are there will be plenty of delectable produce on hand that will have you reconsidering your weekly menu plans. Flexibility is key not only to finding the best produce but in eating the best produce as well.

Plan ahead: If you don't plan to go straight home from the market, take a cooler so that fresh items won't spoil in a warm car.

Bring cash: Most vendors appreciate it if you have small bills for purchasing. And while some larger markets will accept credit cards, most will not accept personal checks.

Take your time: Scope out the entire market before making your selections. Prices and types of produce vary among the different vendors. You'll want to shop just as wisely here as anywhere else.

Something old, something new: While having access to the produce you enjoy regularly is important, so is sampling offerings that may be new to you. Educate yourself in the world of food by picking up something you've never tried before and then talking about the product with the local farmer selling it. You'll learn and taste something new!

Take your kids: There's no better way to introduce your children to new foods than letting them take part. Allow kids to talk to the vendors and pick out some produce.

Talk to the farmers: Make connections with the local farmers in your area. You might glean some unique cooking tips or even recipe ideas.

Bright is best: Look for blemish-free, brightly colored fruits and vegetables. Any bruised or damaged produce will spoil quickly.

More than just produce: While farmers markets have traditionally been known for selling fruits and vegetables alone, these days many offer one-stop shopping. A variety of organically fed, free-range meats and eggs; fresh-from-the-farm dairy products; canned and preserved items; and home-baked goodies line the interior walls surrounding their field-fresh picks. You'll even find fresh flowers and potted herbs.

Recycle, reduce, reuse: You're already a steward of the environment by shopping at your local farmers market, so remember to take it one step further and bring your own canvas bags, baskets, or boxes to carry away your purchases for the day.

Don't wash right away: Wash fresh produce just before cooking or serving—not before storing.

Join a CSA: If your schedule doesn't allow for a trip to the market, consider joining Community Supported Agriculture. You'll receive regular deliveries of locally grown produce in its prime. Find one nearby at www.localharvest.org.

how to use this book

Cooking by the Season

Take a stroll through our *Farmers Market Cookbook* as we guide you to the freshest, most natural approach to cooking for spring, summer, autumn, and winter. Each seasonal recipe chapter offers Tips From the Farm with an assortment of farmers' advice on purchasing, storing, and using ingredients and produce featured within the recipes. In addition, we've compiled the best tips from our kitchens as complementary cooking techniques for farm-fresh fruits, vegetables, meats, and dairy products. Each chapter also offers the chance to learn a little more about farming and local produce with chef and farmer profiles found on pages 51, 120, 192, and 241.

Know What To Buy When

Use our fresh produce and herb primer beginning on page 264 to assist you in choosing the best produce at the right time of year and getting the most flavor from your foods. You'll find all the information you'll need for selecting, storing, and preparing herbs, fruits, and vegetables according to their seasonal availability.

Locating Your Local Farmers Market

Turn to page 278 for a guide to dozens of farmers markets across the South. Whether you're searching for local markets outside your very own back door or simply browsing to find farmers market stands to visit while traveling, use our resources list to learn more about Southern farmers markets, food festivals, fruit stands, and other local harvest organizations, locations, and Web sites.

spring recipes

Lime-Raspberry Bites

prep: 15 min.

Fruits rich in color, such as raspberries, not only add brightness to your plate, but they are also great ways to boost your health and well-being.

1 (8-oz.) container soft light cream cheese
½ cup powdered sugar
1 tsp. lime zest
1 Tbsp. fresh lime juice
2 (2.1-oz.) packages frozen mini-phyllo pastry shells, thawed
28 fresh raspberries
1 tsp. powdered sugar

1. Stir together first 4 ingredients in a small bowl. Spoon cream cheese mixture evenly into pastry shells. Top each with 1 raspberry. Dust evenly with 1 tsp. powdered sugar just before serving. **Yield:** 28 tartlets.

Orange-Raspberry Bites: Substitute equal amounts orange zest and orange juice for lime zest and lime juice. Prepare recipe as directed.

tips from the farm

Raspberries 101 An intensely flavored fruit, raspberries are made up of many tiny individual sections, each with its own seed, surrounding a central core. It's sweet, slightly acidic flavor makes raspberries suited for eating fresh or for cooking in jams, tarts, pies, snacks, or other desserts. Fresh raspberries are available May through November, but they can also be purchased canned or frozen. Store fresh raspberries in an airtight container in the refrigerator for 2 to 3 days, rinsing lightly before serving.

Salted Caramel Strawberries

prep: 15 min. • **other: 15 min.**

20 large fresh strawberries

40 caramels

3 Tbsp. whipping cream

¼ tsp. salt

1¼ cups coarsely chopped
   mixed nuts

Wax paper

1. Pat strawberries completely dry with paper towels.

2. Microwave caramels, 3 Tbsp. whipping cream, and ¼ tsp. salt in a 1-qt. microwave-safe bowl at MEDIUM (50% power) 3½ minutes or until smooth, stirring at 1-minute intervals.

3. Dip each strawberry halfway into caramel mixture. Roll in nuts, and place on lightly greased wax paper. Let stand 15 minutes. Serve immediately, or cover and chill up to 8 hours. **Yield:** 20 strawberries.

note: For testing purposes only, we used Kraft Caramels and Planters NUTrition Heart Healthy Mix.

One bite of this simple confection will explain the reason for today's craze for salted sweets. Adding a smidgen of salt to melted caramels does the trick.

Grilled Fresh Artichokes

prep: 20 min. · **cook: 45 min.** · **other: 15 min.**

Delicately flavored butters and mayonnaises add interest as dipping sauces while allowing the freshness of the grilled artichokes to shine through.

1 lemon, thinly sliced
5 fresh parsley sprigs
3 garlic cloves
2 tsp. salt
4 fresh artichokes
   (about ¾ lb. each)
3 Tbsp. olive oil
Salt and pepper
Garnish: fresh flat-leaf parsley
   sprigs

Buttery Dipping Sauces:

Balsamic-Apricot Butter
Peppy Basil Butter

Mayo Mixtures:

Chipotle-Lime Mayo
Garlic-Lemon Mayo
Herb-Shallot Mayo
Pepperoncini Mayo

1. Combine lemon, next 3 ingredients, and 2½ cups water in large Dutch oven. Place a steamer basket in Dutch oven.

2. Wash artichokes by plunging up and down in cold water. Cut off stem ends, and trim about 1 inch from top of each artichoke, using a serrated knife. Remove any loose bottom leaves. Trim one-fourth off top from each outer leaf, using kitchen shears.

3. Arrange artichokes in steamer basket. Bring to a boil; cover, reduce heat, and simmer 35 to 40 minutes or until stem end is easily pierced with a long wooden pick. Remove artichokes from Dutch oven. Let cool 15 minutes.

4. Preheat grill to 350° to 400° (medium-high). Carefully cut artichokes in half lengthwise; remove and discard choke. Liberally brush cut sides of artichokes with olive oil, and sprinkle with desired amount of salt and pepper.

5. Grill artichokes, covered with grill lid, over 350° to 400° (medium-high) heat 5 minutes on each side. Serve with Buttery Dipping Sauces or Mayo Mixtures. Garnish, if desired. **Yield:** 4 to 8 servings.

buttery dipping sauces

Balsamic-Apricot Butter

You can brush either of these dipping sauces on steamed artichoke halves in place of olive oil, salt, and pepper before grilling.

1. Microwave ⅓ cup butter in a microwave-safe glass bowl at HIGH 30 to 45 seconds or until melted and hot. Stir in 2 Tbsp. apricot preserves and 1 Tbsp. balsamic vinegar. Season with salt and pepper to taste. **Yield:** about ⅓ cup.

Peppy Basil Butter

1. Microwave ⅓ cup butter in a microwave-safe glass bowl at HIGH 30 to 45 seconds or until melted and hot. Stir in 3 Tbsp. chopped fresh basil, ½ tsp. salt, and ¼ tsp. dried crushed red pepper. Let stand 10 minutes before serving. **Yield:** about ⅓ cup.

mayo mixtures

Chipotle-Lime Mayo

1. Stir together ⅔ cup mayonnaise, 1 Tbsp. minced canned chipotle pepper in adobo sauce, 1 tsp. lime zest, and 2 tsp. lime juice. Season with salt and pepper to taste. **Yield:** about ¾ cup.

Garlic-Lemon Mayo

1. Stir together ⅔ cup mayonnaise, 1 pressed garlic clove, 2 tsp. lemon zest, 1 Tbsp. lemon juice, and ⅛ tsp. ground red pepper. Season with salt to taste. **Yield:** about ¾ cup.

Herb-Shallot Mayo

1. Stir together ⅔ cup mayonnaise, 2 Tbsp. finely chopped fresh flat-leaf parsley, 1 Tbsp. Dijon mustard, and 1 minced shallot. Season with salt and pepper to taste. **Yield:** about ¾ cup.

Pepperoncini Mayo

1. Stir together ⅔ cup mayonnaise, 3 Tbsp. chopped pepperoncini peppers, and 1 tsp. lemon zest. Season with salt and pepper to taste. **Yield:** about ¾ cup.

Also try these flavored mayonnaises with Cornmeal-Fried Artichokes (page 49). They're great as sandwich spreads, tossed with cooked pasta for pasta salad, as sauces for grilled vegetables, or slathered on fresh corn on the cob.

Guacamole–Goat Cheese Toasts

prep: 15 min. · **cook: 6 min.** · **other: 30 min.**

2   ripe avocados
3   Tbsp. finely chopped red
     onion, divided
½   medium-size jalapeño pepper,
     seeded and chopped
1   garlic clove, pressed
2½   tsp. fresh lime juice
¼   tsp. salt
¼   tsp. coarsely ground pepper
½   cup crumbled goat cheese
1   fresh tomatillo, husk removed
1   (7-oz.) package miniature
     white pita rounds
2   Tbsp. olive oil
1   plum tomato, seeded and
     finely chopped

1. Cut avocados in half. Scoop pulp into a bowl, and mash with a potato masher or fork until slightly chunky. Stir in 2 Tbsp. red onion and next 5 ingredients. Gently fold in cheese. Place plastic wrap directly on surface of mixture, and let stand at room temperature 30 minutes.

2. Meanwhile, preheat oven to 375°. Finely chop tomatillo.

3. Separate pita rounds lengthwise into two halves. Arrange in a single layer on a baking sheet; drizzle with olive oil.

4. Bake at 375° for 6 to 8 minutes or until toasted. Top each with 1 rounded teaspoonful avocado mixture. Stir together tomatillo, tomato, and remaining 1 Tbsp. red onion. Top avocado mixture with tomatillo mixture. Sprinkle with coarsely ground pepper to taste. **Yield:** about 10 appetizer servings.

note: For testing purposes only, we used Toufayan Bakeries Mini Pitettes.

Goat cheese comes in several forms, from creamy spreads to drier crumbles. The crumbled variety works best for this recipe.

tips from the farm

Avocado Care Avocados are a tropical fruit grown mostly in Florida and California. This fruit is known for its lush, buttery texture and mild, nutlike flavor. Some avocados are rock hard when purchased. Place these in a paper bag and leave at room temperature; they'll soften in 2 to 5 days. Refrigerate ripe avocados and use within a few days. Avocados don't freeze well.

Beef-and-Asparagus Bundles

prep: 20 min. • **cook: 1 min.**

Use chives to tie together these simple appetizers for a fresh-from-the-garden finishing touch.

16 asparagus spears
1 (4-oz.) package garlic-and-herb spreadable cheese
2 heads Bibb lettuce, leaves separated
8 thin slices deli roast beef, halved
1 red bell pepper, cut into 16 strips
16 fresh chives (optional)

1. Snap off and discard tough ends of asparagus. Cut asparagus tips into 3½-inch pieces, reserving any remaining end portions for another use.

2. Cook asparagus in boiling water to cover 1 to 2 minutes or until crisp-tender; drain. Plunge into ice water to stop the cooking process; drain and pat dry with paper towels.

3. Spoon cheese into a 1-qt. zip-top plastic freezer bag. (Do not seal.) Snip 1 corner of bag to make a small hole, and pipe cheese down center of each lettuce leaf. Arrange 1 roast beef slice, 1 asparagus spear, and 1 red bell pepper strip in each lettuce leaf. If desired, wrap sides of lettuce around roast beef and vegetables, and tie bundles with chives. **Yield:** 16 bundles (8 appetizer servings).

note: For testing purposes only, we used Alouette Garlic & Herbs and Boar's Head Londonport Seasoned Roast Beef.

tips from our kitchen

Storing and Cooking Use fresh asparagus as soon as possible. Store stalk side down in a glass of water; cover with plastic wrap, and refrigerate. Before cooking, remove and discard the tough ends of asparagus spears. The easiest way to do this is to bend the stem end until it snaps. It will snap where the most tender part begins.

Lemon-Dill Chicken Salad–Stuffed Eggs

prep: 30 min. ◦ **cook: 12 min.** ◦ **other: 1 hr., 45 min.**

2¼ lb. skinned and boned
    chicken breasts
1½ tsp. salt, divided
½ tsp. freshly ground pepper
24 large hard-cooked eggs,
    peeled
1   cup mayonnaise
2   green onions, finely chopped
1   Tbsp. chopped fresh parsley
1   Tbsp. chopped fresh dill
2   Tbsp. fresh lemon juice

1. Sprinkle chicken evenly with 1 tsp. salt and ½ tsp. pepper. Grill, covered with grill lid, over high heat (400° to 500°) 6 to 8 minutes on each side or until done. Let stand 15 minutes; cover and chill at least 30 minutes.

2. Slice hard-cooked eggs in half lengthwise; carefully remove yolks, keeping egg white halves intact. Reserve yolks for another use.

3. Stir together mayonnaise, next 4 ingredients, and remaining ½ tsp. salt in a large bowl.

4. Pulse cooled chicken in a food processor 3 to 4 times or until shredded; stir into mayonnaise mixture until blended. Spoon chicken mixture evenly into egg white halves. Cover and chill at least 1 hour. **Yield:** 48 appetizers.

Grilling the chicken adds a nice smoky flavor to such a simple recipe; however, 5 cups shredded cooked chicken can be substituted. Lemon-Dill Chicken Salad can be stored in the refrigerator in an airtight container for up to three days.

Minted Lemon Iced Tea

prep: 5 min. · **other: 2 hr., 5 min.**

Adjust the amount of sugar in the tea to suit your taste buds. Or omit the sugar, and serve unsweetened tea with Simple Syrup. Keep Simple Syrup on hand in the refrigerator to stir into iced tea or cocktails. The sugar is already dissolved, so the syrup blends in easily.

2 qt. boiling water
10 lemon zinger tea bags
1 to 1½ cups sugar (optional)
1 cup fresh mint leaves
Simple Syrup (optional)

1. Pour boiling water over tea bags. Stir in sugar, if desired, and mint; steep 5 minutes. Remove tea bags and mint leaves. Chill 2 hours. Stir in Simple Syrup, if desired. **Yield:** 2 qt.

simple syrup

prep: 2 min. · **cook: 5 min.**

½ cup water
½ cup sugar

1. Bring water and sugar to a boil over medium-high heat in a saucepan, stirring until sugar dissolves; boil 1 minute. Remove from heat; cool. Cover and chill until ready to serve. Stir desired amount into tea. **Yield:** ¾ cup (enough for 12 drinks).

Kiwi-Lemonade Spritzer

prep: 10 min.

4 kiwifruit, peeled
1 (12-oz.) can frozen lemonade concentrate, thawed and undiluted
3 cups lemon-lime soft drink, chilled

1. Cut kiwifruit into chunks. Process fruit chunks and lemonade concentrate in a food processor until smooth, stopping to scrape down sides.
2. Pour mixture through a wire-mesh strainer into a pitcher, discarding solids. Stir in lemon-lime soft drink just before serving. **Yield:** 5 cups.

Strawberry-Kiwi-Lemonade Spritzer: Process 2 cups fresh strawberries; 4 kiwifruit, peeled and cut into chunks; and 1 (12-oz.) can frozen lemonade concentrate, thawed and undiluted, in a food processor until smooth, stopping to scrape down sides. Proceed as directed. **Yield:** 5 cups.

Minted Lemon
Iced Tea

Lemonade with
Lime Ice Cubes

Lemonade

prep: 10 min. • **cook: 5 min.**

1   to 1½ cups sugar
1   Tbsp. lemon zest (about
     2 lemons)
1½ cups fresh lemon juice
     (about 13 lemons)
7   cups ice water

1. Bring ½ cup water to a boil in a medium sauce-pan. Stir in sugar and lemon zest, stirring until sugar is dissolved; remove from heat. Stir in lemon juice and ice water. **Yield:** 2½ qt.

Limeade: Substitute 1 Tbsp. lime zest for lemon zest and 1½ cups fresh lime juice for lemon juice, and proceed with recipe as directed.

To extract the most juice from lemons, microwave them at HIGH for about 15 seconds. Get double-duty from lemons by removing the zest before squeezing the juice. To remove the zest, use a special zester or fine grater (such as the Microplane Food Grater, which peels several strips at a time).

Lime Ice Cubes

prep: 10 min. • **other: 8 hr.**

2   medium limes
1   qt. cold water
¼   cup fresh lime juice

1. Cut each lime into ¼-inch-thick slices; cut each slice into 4 wedges.
2. Stir together 1 qt. cold water and ¼ cup lime juice. Fill each compartment of 3 ice cube trays evenly with lime juice mixture. Place 1 lime wedge in each ice cube compartment. Freeze 8 hours or until firm. **Yield:** 42 ice cubes.

Orange-Pineapple Smoothie

prep: 5 min.

2   cups frozen pineapple chunks
1   cup orange juice
1   cup vanilla yogurt
¾   cup milk
¼   cup no-calorie sweetener,
     granular
Garnish: orange wedges

1. Process frozen pineapple chunks and next 4 ingredients in a blender until smooth, stopping to scrape down sides. Garnish, if desired; serve immediately. **Yield:** about 4¼ cups.

Chicken Tortellini With Asparagus and Olives

prep: 15 min. • **cook: 8 min.**

This pasta dish gets a flavor-filled makeover with colorful veggies. Add a green salad tossed with a light vinaigrette, and dinner's on the table in under 30 minutes.

1 (20-oz.) package refrigerated herb-and-chicken tortellini
1 lb. fresh asparagus
¼ cup chopped green onions (about 2 onions)
2 Tbsp. olive oil
1 medium-size red bell pepper, cut into thin strips
1 (10-oz.) jar sun-dried tomato pesto
¼ cup (1 oz.) shredded Parmesan cheese
2 to 3 Tbsp. sliced ripe black olives (optional)

1. Prepare tortellini according to package directions.
2. Meanwhile, snap off and discard tough ends of asparagus. Cut asparagus into 2-inch pieces.
3. Sauté onions in hot oil in a large skillet over medium heat 1 to 2 minutes or until softened. Increase heat to medium-high, add asparagus and bell pepper, and sauté 5 to 6 minutes.
4. Stir in pesto. Cook, stirring occasionally, 2 to 3 minutes or until thoroughly heated. Remove from heat; stir in pasta, and sprinkle with Parmesan cheese and, if desired, sliced black olives. Serve immediately. **Yield:** 4 to 6 servings.

Chicken and Pasta With Vegetables: Substitute ½ (16-oz.) package farfalle (bow-tie pasta) for tortellini. Cut 1 lb. chicken breast tenders into bite-size pieces, and sprinkle with 1 tsp. salt and ½ tsp. freshly ground pepper. Sauté chicken in 2 Tbsp. hot oil in a large skillet over medium-high heat 6 to 7 minutes or until done. Proceed with recipe as directed, stirring in chicken with pasta in Step 4.

tips from the farm

Enjoying Peppers Though classified as a fruit, peppers are enjoyed as a vegetable and a seasoning. The sweet varieties, such as red bell peppers, are mild-flavored. Bell peppers can be stored in a plastic bag in the refrigerator up to a week.

Chicken Enchiladas

prep: 15 min.   •   **cook:** 35 min.

3   cups chopped cooked chicken
2   cups (8 oz.) shredded
     Monterey Jack cheese with
     peppers
½   cup sour cream
1   (4.5-oz.) can chopped green
     chiles, drained
⅓   cup chopped fresh cilantro
8   (8-inch) flour tortillas
Vegetable cooking spray
1   (8-oz.) container sour cream
1   (8-oz.) jar tomatillo salsa
Toppings: diced tomatoes,
     chopped avocado, chopped
     green onions, sliced ripe
     olives, chopped fresh cilantro

1. Preheat oven to 350°. Stir together first 5 ingredients. Spoon chicken mixture evenly down center of each tortilla, and roll up. Arrange seam side down in a lightly greased 13- x 9-inch baking dish. Coat tortillas with vegetable cooking spray.

2. Bake at 350° for 35 to 40 minutes or until golden brown.

3. Stir together 8-oz. container sour cream and salsa. Spoon over hot enchiladas; sprinkle with desired toppings. **Yield:** 4 servings.

Garden-fresh toppings, such as tomatoes, chopped avocado, green onions, and cilantro, transform this favorite entrée into a feast of refreshing flavors. They make pretty garnishes, or you can set up little serving bowls for them and let everyone choose their favorite toppings to add to individual servings.

Strawberry-Turkey-Brie Panini

prep: 15 min. • **cook: 2 min. per batch.**

To prepare these sandwiches without a panini press, cook them in a preheated grill pan over medium-high heat 2 to 3 minutes on each side or until golden.

1 (8-oz.) Brie round
8 Italian bread slices
8 oz. thinly sliced smoked turkey
8 fresh basil leaves
½ cup sliced fresh strawberries
2 Tbsp. red pepper jelly
2 Tbsp. butter, melted
Garnish: strawberry halves

1. Trim and discard rind from Brie. Cut Brie into ½-inch-thick slices. Layer 4 bread slices evenly with turkey, basil leaves, strawberries, and Brie.
2. Spread 1½ tsp. pepper jelly on 1 side of each of remaining 4 bread slices; place bread slices, jelly sides down, on top of Brie. Brush sandwiches with melted butter.
3. Cook sandwiches, in batches, in a preheated panini press 2 to 3 minutes or until golden brown. Garnish, if desired. **Yield:** 4 servings.

note: For testing purposes only, we used Braswell's Red Pepper Jelly.

tips from our kitchen

"Hulling" Strawberries Before you slice, cut in half, puree, or chop strawberries for a recipe, you should "hull." This term means removing the leaves and tiny core beneath the cap of the berry. A paring knife will do it, but be careful not to remove too much fruit. To use a tweezer-like strawberry huller (available at kitchen shops), pinch the berry right beneath the cap and twist.

Ham-Swiss-and-Asparagus Sandwiches

prep: 20 min. • **cook: 4 min.**

¾ lb. fresh asparagus
3 Tbsp. butter, softened
1 small garlic clove, minced
4 (6-inch) French bread loaves, split
3 Tbsp. mayonnaise
8 Baked Glazed Ham slices
4 Swiss cheese slices*
Green leaf lettuce
3 plum tomatoes, sliced

1. Snap off tough ends of asparagus. Cook in boiling water to cover 3 minutes or until crisp-tender; drain. Plunge into ice water to stop the cooking process; drain and chill.
2. Stir together butter and garlic.
3. Spread butter mixture evenly over bottom halves of bread. Spread mayonnaise evenly over top halves of bread. Layer bottom halves evenly with ham, asparagus, and cheese; place on a baking sheet.
4. Broil 2 inches from heat 1 minute or just until cheese melts. Top evenly with lettuce, tomato, and top halves of bread. **Yield:** 4 servings.

*Substitute 6 oz. thinly sliced Brie with rind removed for Swiss cheese slices, if desired.

No time to bake a ham? Purchase ¾ lb. sliced deli ham instead to substitute for the Baked Glazed Ham.

baked glazed ham

prep: 10 min. • **cook: 1 hr., 30 min.** • **other: 15 min.**

2 Tbsp. sugar
1 Tbsp. paprika
1 Tbsp. chili powder
1 tsp. ground cumin
¾ tsp. ground cinnamon
½ tsp. ground cloves
1 (8-lb.) smoked fully cooked ham half, trimmed
1 (12-oz.) can cola soft drink
1 (8-oz.) jar plum or apricot preserves
⅓ cup orange juice

1. Preheat oven to 325°. Combine first 6 ingredients. Score fat on ham in a diamond pattern. Sprinkle ham with sugar mixture, and place in a lightly greased shallow roasting pan. Pour cola into pan.
2. Bake, covered, at 325° for 1 hour. Uncover and bake 15 more minutes.
3. Stir together preserves and orange juice. Spoon ¾ cup glaze over ham; bake 15 more minutes or until a meat thermometer inserted into thickest portion registers 140°. Let stand 15 minutes before slicing. Serve with remaining glaze. **Yield:** 16 servings.

French Onion Soup

prep: 20 min. • **cook: 1 hr., 4 min.**

This recipe for the most popular kind of onion soup blends both chicken broth and beef consommé for a richly satisfying soup.

¼ cup butter
5 medium-size white onions, thinly sliced (about 3 lb.)
1 (32-oz.) container chicken broth
2 (10½-oz.) cans beef consommé
¼ cup dry white wine
3 fresh thyme sprigs
2 fresh parsley sprigs
Salt and freshly ground pepper to taste
6 (¾-inch-thick) French baguette slices
6 (1-oz.) Swiss cheese slices
Garnish: fresh thyme sprigs

1. Melt butter in a Dutch oven over medium-high heat; add onion, and cook, stirring often, 40 minutes or until golden.
2. Add chicken broth and next 4 ingredients; bring to a boil. Reduce heat, and simmer, stirring occasionally, 20 minutes. Remove and discard herbs. Add salt and pepper to taste.
3. Ladle into 6 ovenproof bowls; top with bread and cheese slices. Broil 5½ inches from heat 4 minutes or until cheese is browned and bubbly. Garnish, if desired. **Yield:** 6 servings.

tips from our kitchen

Handling Onions To rid hands of an "oniony" smell, rub them with a little lemon juice, or try rubbing fingertips on the bowl of a stainless steel spoon under warm, running water or rubbing hands over the stainless kitchen faucet.

Fresh Asparagus Soup

prep: 15 min. • **cook: 25 min.** • **other: 10 min.**

1   lb. fresh asparagus
2   cups low-sodium fat-free
    chicken broth
½   cup chopped onion
1   garlic clove, chopped
¾   tsp. fresh thyme, divided
1   Tbsp. all-purpose flour
2   cups 1% low-fat milk
2   tsp. butter
½   tsp. salt
½   tsp. lemon zest, divided
½   cup reduced-fat sour cream
1   Tbsp. fresh lemon juice
Garnish: fresh thyme sprig

1. Snap off and discard tough ends of asparagus. Cut asparagus into 2-inch pieces.
2. Combine asparagus, broth, onion, garlic, and ½ tsp. thyme in a large saucepan over medium-high heat; bring to a boil. Reduce heat to medium-low; cover and simmer 10 minutes. Remove from heat; let stand 10 minutes. Process asparagus mixture, in batches, in a blender or food processor until smooth. Return to pan.
3. Whisk together flour and milk until smooth. Gradually add flour mixture to asparagus mixture, whisking until blended. Bring to a boil, stirring constantly. Reduce heat; simmer, stirring constantly, 5 minutes. Remove from heat; stir in butter, salt, ¼ tsp. lemon zest, and remaining ¼ tsp. thyme.
4. Combine sour cream, lemon juice, and remaining ¼ tsp. lemon zest. Top each serving with about 5 tsp. sour cream mixture. Garnish, if desired. **Yield:** 4 servings.

tips from the farm

Green vs. White Long asparagus spears are most often green, but sometimes white, with slightly pinkish buds on the tips. Asparagus has a mild flavor and delicate texture that becomes tougher as it ages. Most asparagus sold in the United States are green, but Europeans favor white asparagus, which have been kept covered underground while growing and therefore don't turn green.

Tropical Fruit Medley

prep: 25 min. • **other: 30 min.**

A large bowl filled with ice makes a fun serving idea for small glasses of this refreshing soup. It's also pretty served in a shallow, wide-rimmed bowl.

1   fresh pineapple, peeled, cored, and chopped
2   fresh mangoes, peeled and chopped
3   kiwifruit, peeled and chopped
¼   lb. green seedless grapes, halved (about 1 cup)
¼   tsp. ground cardamom
4   cups white grape juice
Garnish: fresh mint sprigs

1. Stir together first 4 ingredients in a large bowl. Sprinkle with cardamom.
2. Pour grape juice over fruit, stirring gently. Cover and chill 30 minutes. Garnish, if desired. **Yield:** 12 servings.

Chilled Strawberry Soup

prep: 10 min. • **other: 2 hr.**

Garnish this creamy milk shake of a soup with chopped strawberries for added appeal.

1   (16-oz.) container fresh strawberries, sliced
2   cups half-and-half
1¼ cups sour cream
¾   cup powdered sugar
2   Tbsp. white balsamic vinegar

1. Process strawberries in a food processor until smooth, stopping to scrape down sides as needed; pour into a large bowl. Whisk in half-and-half and remaining ingredients. Cover and chill at least 2 hours or up to 3 days. Stir just before serving. **Yield:** 4 to 5 servings.

Lightened Chilled Strawberry Soup: Substitute 2 cups fat-free half-and-half and 1¼ cups light sour cream for regular. Proceed with recipe as directed.

Tropical Fruit Medley

Cornmeal-Fried Artichokes

prep: 30 min. • **cook: 5 min. per batch.**

4 fresh artichokes (about ¾ lb. each)

Canola oil

1½ cups plain yellow cornmeal

2 tsp. kosher salt

1½ tsp. fresh ground pepper

¾ cup buttermilk

1 large egg

¾ cup all-purpose flour

Mayo Mixtures:
(recipes on page 23)

Chipotle-Lime Mayo
Garlic-Lemon Mayo
Herb-Shallot Mayo
Pepperoncini Mayo

1. Cut 3 inches from top of each artichoke, using a serrated knife. Discard top portion. Remove and discard leaves from bottom portions of artichokes. Trim green skin from sides and stems, using a paring knife, being careful to leave stem ends intact. Cut each artichoke lengthwise into fourths. Remove and discard chokes.
2. Pour oil to a depth of 3 inches into a Dutch oven; heat over medium-high heat to 350°.
3. Combine cornmeal, salt, and pepper in a shallow bowl. Whisk together buttermilk and egg in another bowl.
4. Toss artichokes in flour. Dip in egg mixture, and dredge in cornmeal mixture, shaking off excess.
5. Fry artichokes, in batches, in hot oil 5 minutes or until tender and golden brown. Drain on a wire rack over paper towels. Serve with Mayo Mixtures. **Yield:** 3 to 4 servings.

Fast Fried Artichokes: Substitute 2 (14-oz.) cans artichoke bottoms, rinsed and drained, for fresh artichokes. Reduce salt to 1 tsp. Pat artichokes dry with paper towels; cut each into fourths. Proceed with recipe as directed, beginning with Step 2.

These are a delightful surprise and worth the time. You really do remove all the leaves. This is based on the Italian fritto misto, or mixed fry, that includes small pieces of battered and fried meats, fish, and vegetables, especially artichokes. Keep fried artichokes warm between batches on a jelly-roll pan in a 225° oven for up to 30 minutes.

tips from the farm

Buying Artichokes An artichoke is the flowering bud of a thistle plant. For top-quality plants, choose artichokes that are heavy for their size, bright, almost shiny green with a purple tinge, cold but not wet feeling, and have tightly compacted leaves. Peak season for artichokes is between March and May. They're most economical during this time.

Asparagus–New Potato Hash

prep: 20 min.   •   cook: 21 min.   •   other: 15 min.

Hash is traditionally made with finely chopped meat and potatoes. Fresh asparagus makes a colorful, garden-fresh variation.

1 lb. small red potatoes
1 lb. fresh asparagus
2 shallots, minced
2 Tbsp. olive oil
1 tsp. chopped fresh thyme
1 tsp. salt
½ tsp. pepper
2 tsp. fresh lemon juice
⅓ cup crumbled farmer's cheese or queso fresco
Garnish: lemon slices

1. Bring potatoes and salted water to cover to a boil in a Dutch oven over medium-high heat. Cook 15 minutes or just until tender; drain well. Cool 15 minutes; cut into quarters.
2. Snap off and discard tough ends of asparagus. Cut asparagus into ½-inch pieces.
3. Sauté shallots in hot oil in a large nonstick skillet 1 minute. Add asparagus, thyme, salt, pepper, and lemon juice; sauté 2 to 3 minutes or until asparagus is crisp-tender. Add potatoes, and sauté 3 minutes or until mixture is thoroughly heated. Remove from heat, and sprinkle with cheese. Garnish, if desired.
Yield: 8 servings.

note: For testing purposes only, we used Chapel Hill Creamery farmer's cheese.

Amy Tornquist, Chef

Watts Grocery, Durham, North Carolina

We bet, as a child, Amy Tornquist made her parents finish their vegetables. Follow her around for more than a minute, especially at the Carrboro Farmers' Market just outside of Chapel Hill, North Carolina, and you can easily imagine her happily encouraging her mom to try one more forkful of "yummy" cauliflower or "awesome" carrots. This gifted chef, busy mother of two, and longtime champion of local food is passionate about produce.

"Even in this economy, it still pays to buy local," insists Amy. The majority of the dairy and vegetables she uses at her restaurant, Watts Grocery, come from within a two-hour radius of Durham, and she has been recognized for her commitment to sustainable agriculture. For example, at her restaurant Amy features cheeses from Elodie Farms in Rougemont, home to Dave Artigues and his farmstead goat cheese-making facility.

"When it comes to feeding my family, I get the most bang for my buck with local or organic produce. That's my top priority," Amy reveals. After that, she considers eggs and then dairy the best values. "Having said that, if it's a decision between buying organic at the grocery store or fresh from your local farmers' market, always go with local first," she recommends. But at the end of the day, Amy says one of the simplest ways to save money and still eat well is to buy in season.

Green Peas With Crispy Bacon

prep: 20 min. • **cook: 17 min.**

6 cups shelled fresh sweet green peas*
4 bacon slices
2 shallots, sliced
1 tsp. orange zest
1 cup fresh orange juice
1 tsp. pepper
½ tsp. salt
2 to 3 Tbsp. chopped fresh mint
1 Tbsp. butter

1. Cook peas in boiling water to cover 5 minutes; drain and set aside.
2. Meanwhile, cook bacon in a large skillet over medium heat until crisp. Remove and crumble bacon; reserve 2 tsp. drippings in skillet.
3. Sauté shallots in hot drippings over medium-high heat 2 minutes or until tender. Stir in orange zest, orange juice, pepper, and salt. Cook, stirring occasionally, 5 minutes or until reduced by half. Add peas, and cook 5 minutes; stir in mint and butter.
4. Transfer peas to a serving dish, and sprinkle with crumbled bacon. **Yield:** 10 to 12 servings.

*2 (16-oz.) bags frozen sweet green peas, thawed, may be substituted. No precooking is necessary; just proceed with recipe as directed, adding peas in Step 3.

If you've never tasted fresh green peas, you're in for a treat. Their delicate fresh flavor and crunchy texture is heavenly.

tips from the farm

Keeping Peas Fresh Crunchy and sweet, green peas, also known as English peas or garden peas, are eaten fresh, removed from their pods. The sugar in fresh peas quickly converts to starch, so it's important that they be prepared and eaten as soon as possible after picking, usually within 2 to 3 days; they should be stored in a plastic bag in the refrigerator.

Mushroom-and-Spinach Toss

prep: 20 min. • cook: 14 min.

½ (16-oz.) package farfalle or
    bow-tie pasta
¼ cup pine nuts
2 Tbsp. butter
1 Tbsp. olive oil
1 (8-oz.) package sliced fresh
    mushrooms
¼ cup sun-dried tomatoes in oil,
    drained and coarsely chopped
2 garlic cloves, minced
¼ cup dry white wine
1 (6-oz.) package fresh baby
    spinach, thoroughly washed
¾ tsp. salt
½ tsp. pepper
½ cup freshly grated Parmesan
    cheese

1. Prepare pasta according to package directions.
2. Preheat oven to 350°. Arrange ¼ cup pine nuts in a single layer in a shallow pan. Bake 5 to 7 minutes or until lightly toasted and fragrant.
3. Melt butter with oil in a large skillet over medium-high heat; add mushrooms, and sauté 5 to 6 minutes or until golden brown and most liquid has evaporated. Reduce heat to medium, and add tomatoes and garlic; cook, stirring constantly, 1 to 2 minutes.
4. Stir in wine, and cook 30 seconds, stirring to loosen particles from bottom of skillet. Stir in hot cooked pasta and spinach. Cook, stirring occasionally, 2 to 3 minutes or until spinach is wilted. Stir in salt and pepper. Sprinkle with Parmesan cheese and toasted pine nuts. Serve immediately. **Yield:** 6 servings.

tips from the farm

Cultivated vs. Wild Mushrooms belong to the fungus family and are available in many different varieties. They have a rich, earthy flavor and basically fall into two categories: cultivated and wild. Cultivated mushrooms are commonly found in most supermarkets, but many cooks consider the flavors of wild mushrooms to be more exotic and exciting. It's vitally important to know which species are edible and which are poisonous. Never pick or eat wild mushrooms unless a trained expert collector has identified them. Many markets now carry wild mushrooms that have been professionally farmed and are not poisonous.

Crispy "Fried" Onion Rings

prep: 20 min. · cook: 12 min.

1 large sweet onion
½ cup low fat buttermilk
1 egg white
½ cup all-purpose flour
2 Tbsp. olive oil, divided
Vegetable cooking spray
½ tsp. coarse kosher salt

1. Cut onion into ¼-inch-thick slices, and separate into rings. Select largest 12 rings, reserving remaining onion slices for another use.
2. Preheat oven to 400°. Whisk together buttermilk and egg white in a small bowl until blended.
3. Dredge onion rings in flour; dip into buttermilk mixture, coating well. Dredge again in flour, and place on a baking sheet.
4. Heat 2 tsp. oil in a 10-inch skillet over medium-high heat. Tilt pan to coat bottom of skillet. Add 4 onion rings to skillet, and cook 1 minute on each side or until golden. Wipe skillet clean. Repeat procedure twice with remaining onion rings and oil. Place fried onion rings on an aluminum foil-lined baking sheet coated with cooking spray.
5. Bake at 400° for 3 minutes. Turn onion rings, and bake 3 more minutes. Remove from oven, and sprinkle with salt. Serve immediately. **Yield:** 3 servings.

Cooking the onion rings in oil for a short time gives them a fried flavor without the calories.

how to make "fried" onion rings

1. Dredge onion rings in flour, and dip into buttermilk mixture; then dredge again in flour.
2. Cook 1 minute on each side or until golden. 3. Finish up the rings by baking them at 400° for 3 minutes on each side.

  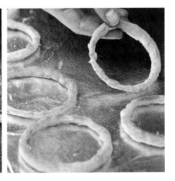

Sweet Onion Pudding

prep: 20 min. • **cook: 1 hr., 5 min.**

½ cup butter

6 medium-size sweet onions, thinly sliced

6 large eggs, lightly beaten

2 cups whipping cream

1 (3-oz.) package shredded Parmesan cheese

3 Tbsp. all-purpose flour

2 Tbsp. sugar

2 tsp. baking powder

1 tsp. salt

Garnish: fresh thyme sprigs

1. Melt butter in a large skillet over medium heat; add onions. Cook, stirring often, 30 to 40 minutes or until caramel colored; remove from heat.

2. Preheat oven to 350°. Whisk together eggs, cream, and Parmesan cheese in a large bowl. Combine flour and next 3 ingredients in a separate bowl; gradually whisk into egg mixture until blended. Stir onions into egg mixture; spoon into a lightly greased 13- x 9-inch baking dish.

3. Bake, uncovered, at 350° for 35 to 40 minutes or until set. Garnish, if desired. **Yield:** 8 servings.

Easy and delicious, this side-dish pudding is a perfect complement to a pork or beef entrée.

tips from the farm

Keeping Them Sweet Vidalia, Walla Walla, Texas Supersweet, and Maui onions are mild, sweet and juicy and named for their place or origin, since, due to soil and climate, they lose their characteristic sweetness if grown elsewhere. Because they are so sweet, they have a shorter storage life than other dry onions. To extend the life of sweet onions, store them so that they aren't touching each other; some cooks hang them in old panty hose with knots tied in between each onion. Stored properly, sweet onions can be kept for 4 to 6 weeks.

Minted Mixed Fruit

prep: 15 min. • other: 2 hr.

The kiwifruit in this recipe are peeled. Other options for enjoying kiwifruit include halving and scooping out the fruit with a tablespoon, peeling and slicing for salads and desserts, or using it as a garnish.

1 qt. strawberries, halved (about 3 cups)
3 cups fresh pineapple chunks
4 kiwifruit, peeled and sliced
1 cup sugar
½ cup pineapple juice
½ cup ginger ale
¼ cup chopped fresh mint

1. Place fruit in a shallow serving bowl. Whisk together sugar, juice, and ginger ale until sugar is dissolved; gently stir in mint, and pour over fruit. Cover and chill 2 hours before serving. **Yield:** 8 to 10 servings.

Tangy Berries-and-Cheese Salad

prep: 10 min. • cook: 5 min.

¼ cup slivered almonds
2 Tbsp. olive oil
2 Tbsp. white balsamic vinegar
¼ tsp. salt
⅛ tsp. coarsely ground pepper
1 Tbsp. thinly sliced fresh basil
1 (5-oz.) package mâche (about 4 cups), thoroughly washed*
1½ cups fresh strawberries, cut in half
½ cup crumbled farmer's cheese**

1. Preheat oven to 350°. Bake almonds in a single layer in a shallow pan 5 to 7 minutes or until toasted and fragrant.
2. Whisk together oil and next 3 ingredients in a bowl; stir in basil. Add mâche; toss to combine. Top with strawberries, farmer's cheese, and toasted almonds. Serve immediately. **Yield:** 4 servings.

*4 cups Bibb lettuce may be substituted.
**Queso fresco may be substituted.

Minted Mixed Fruit

Spring Salad

prep: 20 min. • **cook: 2 min.**

1   lb. fresh asparagus
8   cups baby salad greens, thoroughly washed
2   cups seedless red grapes
8   cooked bacon slices, crumbled
1   (4-oz.) package goat cheese, crumbled
4   green onions, sliced
¼   cup pine nuts
Balsamic vinaigrette

1. Snap off and discard tough ends of asparagus; arrange asparagus in a steamer basket over boiling water. Cover and steam 2 to 4 minutes or until asparagus is crisp-tender. Plunge asparagus into ice water to stop the cooking process; drain and cut into 1-inch pieces.

2. Arrange salad greens on a serving platter; top evenly with asparagus, grapes, and next 4 ingredients. Serve with vinaigrette. **Yield:** 4 servings.

For this recipe, use your favorite brand of bottled balsamic vinaigrette, or make one from scratch as described in the tip box below. Homemade salad dressing is one of those small touches that makes a meal special. Best of all, in 5 minutes flat you can whisk together a batch of delicious vinaigrette that can be stored in the refrigerator for up to 3 to 5 days.

tips from our kitchen

Homemade Vinaigrette To make homemade vinaigrette, all you need is oil, vinegar, salt, pepper, and a jar with a tight-fitting lid. Balsamic vinegar and olive oil is our preferred combination, though cider vinegar, canola oil, and flavored oils such as hazelnut or walnut work well too. Because balsamic is a sweeter tasting vinegar, we like the ratio of 1 part vinegar to 2 parts oil. (The standard ratio for other vinegars is 1 part vinegar to 3 parts oil.) Put these in the jar with the salt and pepper; shake well, and you're done.

Orange, Radish, and Cucumber Salad

prep: 15 min.

3 large navel oranges
1 small bunch radishes, thinly sliced
½ large seedless cucumber, thinly sliced
1 Tbsp. finely chopped fresh mint
1 tsp. olive oil
Salt and freshly ground black pepper to taste

1. Peel oranges; remove and discard white pith. Separate oranges over a bowl into sections, reserving juice. Place orange sections and 2 Tbsp. juice in a serving bowl; gently stir in radishes and next 3 ingredients. Sprinkle with salt and freshly ground pepper to taste. **Yield:** 4 servings.

how to section citrus

1. Using a paring knife, slice away peel and white pith from fruit.
2. Holding fruit over a bowl to catch juice, slice between membrane and one side of fruit segment; then lift segment out with knife.

Rhubarb Upside-Down Cake

prep: 43 min. · **cook: 35 min.** · **other: 5 min.**

¼ cup butter

½ cup chopped pecans

¼ cup firmly packed dark
   brown sugar

1 Tbsp. candied ginger,
   chopped

4 rhubarb stalks (about ½ lb.)

1 (16-oz.) package pound
   cake mix

¾ cup milk

2 large eggs

½ cup sour cream

1 tsp. vanilla extract

Vanilla ice cream (optional)

1. Preheat oven to 350°. Melt butter in a 10½-inch cast-iron skillet over medium heat. Stir in pecans, brown sugar, and candied ginger until sugar dissolves. Remove pecans from pan.

2. Cut 2 rhubarb stalks into 4 (4-inch) pieces; cut each piece lengthwise into thin strips. Chop remaining 2 stalks. Place rhubarb strips into bottom of skillet in a spoke design. Top with pecans and chopped rhubarb.

3. Prepare pound cake mix according to package directions using ¾ cup milk and 2 large eggs; add sour cream and vanilla. Spoon over rhubarb.

4. Bake at 350° for 35 minutes or until a wooden pick inserted in center comes out clean. Let stand 5 minutes on a wire rack. Turn out onto a serving platter; serve with ice cream, if desired. **Yield:** 8 servings.

tips from the farm

Vegetable or Fruit? Rhubarb is a celery-like vegetable that's most commonly cooked and eaten as a fruit. Its long stalks range in color from red to pink, and they are too tart to be eaten raw. In fact, rhubarb is usually cooked with a generous amount of sugar to balance its tartness. After sweetening, it makes delicious sauces, jams, and desserts, and is referred to as "pieplant" because of its popularity as a pie filling.

Strawberries Romanoff Pancakes With Brown Sugar–Sour Cream Sauce

prep: 20 min. • other: 30 min

"Romanoff" is defined as a dessert of strawberries soaked in orange juice or liqueur and topped with whipped cream. Our spin is a sauce inspired by the simple idea of dipping berries in sour cream, then in brown sugar, and eating them immediately.

2   (16-oz.) containers fresh strawberries, sliced (about 6 cups)
⅓   cup granulated sugar
2   Tbsp. orange liqueur*
1   cup sour cream
3   Tbsp. brown sugar
Angela's Pancakes

1. Stir together first 3 ingredients. Cover and let stand 30 minutes.
2. Meanwhile, stir together sour cream and brown sugar. Cover and chill 30 minutes.
3. Stack pancakes on individual plates. Top with strawberry mixture, and dollop with sour cream mixture. Serve immediately. **Yield:** 4 servings.

*Orange juice may be substituted.

note: To make a wonderful shake, puree remaining strawberry mixture in a blender. Add vanilla ice cream and milk; blend to desired thickness.

angela's pancakes

prep: 15 min. • cook: 4 min. per batch. • other: 3 min.

Stand time allows the pancake mixture to thicken and activates the baking soda for light, fluffy results.

1   cup cake flour
1   tsp. baking soda
1   tsp. sugar
1   tsp. orange zest
½   tsp. salt
¾   cup buttermilk
¼   cup milk
1   large egg, lightly beaten
2   Tbsp. butter, melted

1. Combine first 5 ingredients in a large bowl. Whisk together buttermilk, milk, egg, and melted butter; whisk into flour mixture just until blended. Let stand 3 minutes.
2. Pour about ⅛ cup batter for each pancake onto a hot (350°) lightly greased griddle or large nonstick skillet over medium heat. Cook pancakes 2 minutes or until tops are covered with bubbles and edges look dry and cooked. Turn and cook 2 more minutes. Keep pancakes warm in a 200° oven up to 30 minutes. **Yield:** about 18 (2½-inch) pancakes.

summer's bounty

Sweet-and-Salty Honey-Cheese Spread

prep: 10 min.

This easy-to-make spread is ready in 10 minutes—a perfect quick fix for last-minute guests. A generous drizzle of honey is a delicious finishing touch.

1 (10.5-oz.) goat cheese log
½ cup roasted, salted sunflower seeds
⅓ cup honey
1 pt. fresh raspberries, blackberries, or blueberries
Garnish: fresh mint leaves
Assorted crackers

1. Press or roll goat cheese log in sunflower seeds, thoroughly covering cheese, including ends. Arrange cheese on a serving platter with any remaining sunflower seeds. Drizzle with honey. Sprinkle with berries. Garnish, if desired. Serve immediately with assorted crackers. **Yield:** 6 to 8 appetizer servings.

tips from the farm

Tart and Tasty Goat cheese, or chèvre, as you may see it labeled, ranges in texture from moist and creamy to dry and semifirm, and comes in a number of shapes, such as logs and cones. It's available plain or coated with edible ash, herbs, pepper, or leaves. Wrap chèvre in plastic and refrigerate up to 2 weeks.

Guacamole

Guacamole

prep: 10 min. · other: 30 min.

5   ripe avocados
2   Tbsp. finely chopped red
    onion
2   Tbsp. fresh lime juice
½   medium jalapeño pepper,
    seeded and chopped
1   garlic clove, pressed
¾   tsp. salt
Tortilla chips

1. Cut avocados in half. Scoop pulp into a bowl, and mash with a potato masher or fork until slightly chunky. Stir in chopped red onion and next 4 ingredients. Cover with plastic wrap, allowing wrap to touch mixture, and let stand at room temperature 30 minutes. Serve guacamole with tortilla chips. **Yield:** 3½ cups.

Cilantro Guacamole: Mash avocado, and stir in ingredients as directed. Stir in 3 Tbsp. chopped fresh cilantro and an additional 1 Tbsp. lime juice. Cover mixture, and let stand at room temperature 30 minutes.

Prevent refrigerated guacamole from changing color by placing a layer of plastic wrap directly on the surface of the mixture.

Cucumber–Cream Cheese Dip

prep: 19 min. · other: 9 hrs.

5   small cucumbers, unpeeled
½   cup rice vinegar
1   tsp. kosher salt
1   tsp. garlic salt, divided
2   (8-oz.) packages cream
    cheese, softened
½   cup mayonnaise
2   tsp. chopped fresh chives
Garnish: fresh chives
Pita chips

1. Grate cucumbers into a medium bowl. Toss with rice vinegar, salt, and ½ tsp. garlic salt. Cover and chill 8 hours. Drain cucumber mixture well, pressing between paper towels.
2. Beat cream cheese, mayonnaise, and remaining ½ tsp. garlic salt at medium speed with an electric mixer 1 to 2 minutes or until smooth. Stir in cucumber mixture and chives. Cover and chill at least 1 hour. Garnish, if desired, and serve with pita chips. **Yield:** 3 cups.

Stuffed Cherry Tomatoes

prep: 25 min. • **other: 1 hr., 15 min.**

The secret to serving flavorful Stuffed Cherry Tomatoes without having them roll around is to cut a very small slice from the bottom of each tomato.

2   pints cherry tomatoes
1   avocado, peeled and diced
1   tsp. lemon juice
¼   cup mayonnaise
8   cooked bacon slices, crumbled
2   green onions, finely chopped
Salt and pepper to taste

1. Cut a small slice from the top of each tomato; scoop out pulp with a small spoon or melon baller, and discard pulp. Place tomatoes, cut sides down, on paper towels, and let drain 15 minutes.
2. Meanwhile, combine avocado and lemon juice in a small bowl, stirring gently; drain. Stir together mayonnaise, bacon, and green onions; add avocado mixture, and stir gently until combined.
3. Spoon avocado mixture evenly into tomato shells. Cover with plastic wrap, and chill 1 hour. Sprinkle with salt and pepper to taste just before serving.
Yield: 8 servings.

tips from the farm

Fresh is Best Cherry tomatoes are about an inch in diameter and can be red or yellow. Though fresh tomatoes are available year-round, they're at their peak from June through September. There's no comparison between vine-rippened tomatoes and the ones that have been commercially grown, picked green, and artificially ripened; these never come close in texture, aroma, or taste.

Prosciutto-Wrapped Mango Bites

prep: 20 min.

1   ripe mango, peeled
1½ cups loosely packed arugula
¾   cup loosely packed fresh basil
     leaves (about 1 oz.)
4   very thin prosciutto or
     country ham slices
¼   tsp. coarsely ground pepper

1. Cut mango into ¼- to ½-inch slices (about 16). Place 1 mango slice on top of 3 arugula leaves and 1 to 2 basil leaves.

2. Cut each prosciutto slice lengthwise into 4 strips. Wrap center of each mango bundle with 1 prosciutto strip. Arrange on a serving platter, and sprinkle with pepper. **Yield:** 8 appetizer servings.

note: To make ahead, prepare recipe as directed. Cover bites with damp paper towels, and chill 30 minutes.

Prosciutto-Wrapped Melon Bites: Substitute half of 1 small cantaloupe or honeydew for mango. Proceed with recipe as directed.

Prosciutto-Wrapped Pear Bites: Substitute 1 ripe pear, unpeeled, for mango. Cut pear as directed in Step 1. Toss together pear slices and ½ cup lemon-lime soft drink to prevent browning; drain. Proceed with recipe as directed.

Prosciutto-Wrapped Apple Bites: Substitute 1 Gala apple, unpeeled, for mango. Cut apple as directed in Step 1. Toss together apple slices and ½ cup lemon-lime soft drink to prevent browning; drain. Proceed with recipe as directed.

Cold Marinated Shrimp and Avocados

prep: 20 min. • **other: 1 hr.**

Uncooked corn kernels mingle in this marinated salad and contributes to its ultra-fresh flavor.

1   lb. large cooked, peeled shrimp
2   medium avocados, chopped
1   cup fresh corn kernels
¼   cup chopped fresh cilantro
2   Tbsp. chopped red onion
Lime Vinaigrette
Garnishes: fresh cilantro leaves, red onion slices

1. Combine first 5 ingredients. Gently stir in Lime Vinaigrette to coat. Cover and chill at least 1 hour. Garnish, if desired. **Yield:** 8 appetizer servings.

lime vinaigrette

prep: 5 min.

½   cup fresh lime juice
¼   cup honey
1   garlic clove, pressed
½   tsp. salt
¼   tsp. pepper
⅓   cup olive oil

1. Whisk together first 5 ingredients. Gradually whisk in ⅓ cup olive oil until blended. **Yield:** about ¾ cup.

tips from our kitchen

Ready to Serve To make this appetizer ahead, get all the ingredients (except the avocados) ready to combine; place in individual zip-top plastic bags, and store in the refrigerator. Before serving, peel and chop the avocados; gently stir together up to 2 hours before serving, and chill.

Blackberry Iced Tea

prep: 10 min. · **other:** 1 hr.

3 cups fresh or frozen blackberries, thawed
1 cup sugar
1 Tbsp. chopped fresh mint
Pinch of baking soda
4 cups boiling water
3 family-size tea bags
2½ cups cold water or sparkling
   water
Garnishes: fresh blackberries,
   fresh mint sprigs

1. Combine 3 cups blackberries and sugar in large container. Crush blackberries with wooden spoon. Add chopped mint and baking soda. Set aside.
2. Pour 4 cups boiling water over tea bags; cover and let stand 3 minutes. Discard tea bags.
3. Pour tea over blackberry mixture; let stand at room temperature 1 hour. Pour tea through a wire-mesh strainer into a large pitcher, discarding solids. Add 2½ cups cold water, stirring until sugar dissolves. Cover and chill until ready to serve. Garnish, if desired. **Yield:** about 7 cups.

Thread fresh blackberries onto small wooden skewers for eye-catching stirrers that hint at the flavor of the tea.

tips from the farm

Taste of Summer Blackberries are widely cultivated in the United States, and are sometimes called bramble berries because they grow wild on bramble vines along rural roadsides from May through August. They're also available canned and frozen. The only drawback to the blackberry is its fairly large crunchy seeds.

Peach-Mango Daiquiris

prep: 20 min.

Look for cream of coconut in the beverage aisle of your grocery store.

1   (24-oz.) jar mango slices
3   large ripe peaches (about
    1¼ lb.), peeled and chopped*
1   (15-oz.) can cream of coconut
1   (6-oz.) can frozen lemonade
    concentrate, thawed
1½ cups dark rum

1. Drain mango slices, reserving ½ cup liquid. Process mango slices and peaches in a blender until smooth, stopping to scrape down sides. Pour peach mixture into a large container.
2. Process reserved mango liquid, cream of coconut, and lemonade concentrate in blender until smooth. Add coconut mixture and rum to peach mixture, stirring until combined. Use immediately.
3. Process 3 cups peach mixture with 2 cups ice in a blender until smooth. Repeat with remaining peach mixture and ice. **Yield:** about 12 servings.

*1 (20-oz.) bag frozen sliced peaches, thawed, may be substituted.

Peppermint Citrus Cooler

prep: 5 min.

This refreshing treat comes from Baltimore's Flower Mart, held in the Mount Vernon neighborhood. One of the event's most popular traditions, lemon sticks are a zippy combination of half a lemon served with a porous peppermint candy stick as a straw. Sipping the tart juice through the sweet candy cane will bring some zing to your taste buds.

1   lemon, lime, or orange,
    chilled
1   soft peppermint stick

1. Roll 1 chilled lemon, lime, or orange on countertop 3 or 4 times, pressing gently with palm of your hand.
2. Cut a small "X" into top of fruit with a paring knife.
3. Insert 1 soft peppermint candy stick into "X." Sip fruit juice through candy stick. **Yield:** 1 serving.

note: For testing purposes only, we used Bobs Mint Sticks, available from Cracker Barrel Old Country Store. You can also use King Leo Soft Peppermint Sticks, available at www.candycrate.com.

Watermelon Cooler

prep: 30 min. • **other: 8 hr., 15 min.**

8 cups (½-inch) watermelon cubes
1½ cups ginger ale
¼ cup water
1 (6-oz.) can frozen limeade concentrate

1. Place watermelon cubes in a single layer in an extra-large zip-top plastic freezer bag, and freeze 8 hours. Let stand at room temperature 15 minutes.
2. Process half each of watermelon, ginger ale, water, and limeade concentrate in a blender until smooth; pour mixture into a pitcher. Repeat procedure with remaining half of ingredients; stir into pitcher, and serve immediately. **Yield:** about 8 cups.

Honeydew Cooler: Substitute 8 cups (½-inch) honeydew melon cubes for watermelon cubes and 1 (6-oz.) can frozen lemonade concentrate for limeade concentrate. Proceed as directed.

Cantaloupe Cooler: Substitute 8 cups (½-inch) cantaloupe cubes for watermelon, and add 2 tsp. grated fresh ginger to mixture in blender. Proceed as directed.

Coat the glass rims in lime juice, and dip them in lime zest or chopped mint. Spear melon balls on wooden picks for a colorful garnish.

Morning Energizer Smoothie

prep: 10 min.

This great-tasting pick-me-up is packed with vitamins and tastes as rich as a milk shake. Blend one fruit or several with frozen yogurt. Don't forget the orange juice and banana; they add extra sweetness.

- 1 cup vanilla frozen yogurt
- ¾ cup orange juice
- ¾ cup fresh pineapple chunks
- ¾ cup sliced fresh strawberries, frozen
- ¾ cup fresh raspberries
- 1 large banana, sliced and frozen

Additional fresh strawberries (optional)

1. Process all ingredients in a blender until smooth, stopping to scrape down sides as needed. Garnish with additional fresh strawberries, if desired, and serve immediately. **Yield:** 3 to 4 servings.

Green Tea–Kiwi and Mango Smoothie

prep: 15 min.

Chilling the mango mixture in the freezer then layering the kiwi mixture on top gives this good-for-you drink an unusually pretty presentation.

- 2½ cups frozen diced mango
- ¾ cup vanilla fat-free yogurt, divided
- ¼ cup honey, divided
- 2 Tbsp. water
- ½ tsp. lime zest
- 3 ripe kiwifruit, peeled and quartered
- 2 cups ice cubes
- ½ cup packed baby spinach
- 2 Tbsp. bottled green tea

Kiwifruit slices (optional)

1. Place mango, ½ cup yogurt, 2 Tbsp. honey, 2 Tbsp. water, and lime zest in a blender; process until smooth, stirring occasionally. Divide mango mixture into each of 4 serving glasses; place glasses in freezer.
2. Rinse blender container. Place ¼ cup yogurt, 2 Tbsp. honey, kiwifruit, and next 3 ingredients in blender; process until smooth, stirring occasionally. Gently spoon green tea–kiwi mixture onto mango mixture in reserved glasses, working carefully around inside of each glass to create a clean horizontal line. Garnish with kiwifruit slices, and stir to combine flavors, if desired. Serve immediately. **Yield:** 4 servings.

Morning Energizer
Smoothie

Greek-Style Beef and Vegetables

prep: 20 min. • **cook: 10 min.** • **other: 10 min.**

2 lb. (1-inch-thick) boneless top sirloin steak
3 Tbsp. olive oil, divided
2 tsp. kosher salt, divided
1 tsp. freshly ground pepper, divided
6 medium-size yellow squash, cut in half
1 red onion, cut into ½-inch-thick slices
1 lemon, cut in half
1 (10-oz.) box plain couscous
½ (4-oz.) package crumbled feta cheese
Chunky Cucumber-Mint Sauce

1. Preheat grill to 350° to 400° (medium-high). Rub steak with 1 Tbsp. oil, 1½ tsp. kosher salt, and ¾ tsp. pepper.
2. Brush squash and onion with remaining 2 Tbsp. oil; sprinkle with remaining ½ tsp. kosher salt and ¼ tsp. pepper.
3. Grill steak and vegetables, covered with grill lid, over 350° to 400° (medium-high) heat 5 to 7 minutes on each side or until steak reaches desired degree of doneness and vegetables are tender. Remove steak and vegetables from grill; squeeze juice from lemon over steak and vegetables. Cover steak and vegetables with aluminum foil, and let stand 10 minutes.
4. Meanwhile, prepare couscous according to package directions.
5. Cut steak across the grain into thin slices. Cover and chill half of sliced steak (about 1 lb.) up to 2 days. Top couscous with vegetables; sprinkle with feta cheese. Serve with remaining half of steak and Chunky Cucumber-Mint Sauce. **Yield:** 4 servings.

note: This recipe calls for you to grill twice as much meat as you will need, so save half to serve later in the week. It will make wonderful fajitas or steak sandwiches.

chunky cucumber-mint sauce

prep: 10 min.

1 cup plain yogurt
3 Tbsp. sour cream
1 small cucumber, peeled, seeded, and chopped
4 tsp. chopped fresh mint
Salt and pepper to taste

1. Stir together yogurt, sour cream, cucumber, mint, and salt and pepper to taste. **Yield:** about 1¾ cups.

Blueberry-Rum Marinated Pork Tenderloin

prep: 10 min. • cook: 18 min. • other: 4 hrs., 40 min.

2 (1 lb. each) pork tenderloins
1 cup fresh blueberries
¾ cup rum
¼ cup lemon juice
2 garlic cloves
2 Tbsp. brown sugar
1 Tbsp. chopped sweet onion
1 Tbsp. white vinegar
Blueberry Salsa

1. Remove silver skin from tenderloins, leaving a thin layer of fat covering the tenderloins.
2. Process blueberries and next 6 ingredients in a blender or food processor until smooth, stopping to scrape down sides. Pour mixture into large zip-top plastic freezer bag; add pork, turning to coat. Seal and chill at least 4 hours.
3. Preheat grill to 300° to 350° (medium). Remove pork from marinade, discarding marinade. Let stand at room temperature 30 minutes.
4. Grill pork, covered with grill lid, over 300° to 350° (medium) heat 8 to 12 minutes on each side or until a meat thermometer inserted in thickest portion registers 155°. Remove from grill. Loosely cover pork with foil; let stand 10 minutes or until thermometer registers 160°. Cut pork into slices.
Top with Blueberry Salsa. **Yield:** 8 servings.

blueberry salsa

prep: 15 min.

2 cups chopped fresh blueberries
1 cup whole fresh blueberries
⅓ cup diced red bell pepper
¼ cup chopped onion
¼ cup fresh lemon juice
3 Tbsp. chopped fresh mint
2 jalapeño peppers, seeded and minced
½ tsp. kosher salt

1. Stir together all ingredients; cover and chill until ready to serve. **Yield:** about 3 cups.

Molasses-Balsamic Pork Kabobs With Green Tomatoes and Plums

prep: 20 min. • cook: 18 min. • other: 30 min.

8 (12-inch) wooden or metal skewers
1 (1.5-lb.) package pork tenderloin, trimmed and cut into 1½-inch pieces
4 large plums, quartered
2 medium-size green tomatoes, cut into eighths
2 medium-size red onions, cut into eighths
2 tsp. seasoned salt
2 tsp. pepper
½ cup molasses
¼ cup balsamic vinegar

1. Soak wooden skewers in water 30 minutes.
2. Preheat grill to 350° to 400° (medium-high). Thread pork and next 3 ingredients alternately onto skewers, leaving ¼ inch between pieces. Sprinkle kabobs with seasoned salt and pepper. Stir together molasses and vinegar.
3. Grill kabobs, covered with grill lid, over 350° to 400° (medium-high) heat 12 minutes, turning after 6 minutes. Baste kabobs with half of molasses mixture, and grill 3 minutes. Turn kabobs, baste with remaining half of molasses mixture, and grill 3 more minutes or until done. **Yield:** 4 to 6 servings.

Molasses-Balsamic Chicken Kabobs With Green Tomatoes and Plums: Substitute 1½ lb. skinned and boned chicken breasts for pork. Proceed with recipe as directed.

These kabobs caramelize to a smoky sweetness when grilled. For a change of taste, swap apples and partially cooked sweet potatoes for green tomatoes and plums.

Ham-and-Tomato Pie

prep: 20 min. • cook: 25 min. • other: 20 min.

1 (8-oz.) package diced cooked ham

1 green onions, sliced

1 (9-inch) frozen unbaked pie shell

1 Tbsp. Dijon mustard

1 cup (4 oz.) shredded mozzarella cheese, divided

2 medium plum tomatoes, thinly sliced

1 large egg

⅓ cup half-and-half

1 Tbsp. chopped fresh basil

⅛ tsp. pepper

Garnishes: fresh basil sprigs, tomato slices

1. Preheat oven to 425°. Sauté ham and green onions in a large nonstick skillet over medium heat 5 minutes or until ham is brown and any liquid evaporates.

2. Brush bottom of pie shell evenly with mustard; sprinkle with ½ cup mozzarella cheese. Spoon ham mixture evenly over cheese, and top with single layer of sliced tomatoes.

3. Beat egg and half-and-half with a fork until blended; pour over tomatoes. Sprinkle evenly with basil, pepper, and remaining ½ cup cheese.

4. Bake on lowest oven rack at 425° for 20 to 23 minutes or until lightly browned and set. Cool on a wire rack 20 minutes. Cut into wedges to serve; garnish, if desired. **Yield:** 4 to 6 servings.

This quiche-like pie is equally yummy for brunch or lunch. You can prepare it with packaged chopped ham or leftover ham.

tips from our kitchen

Perfect Preparation For best results, we don't suggest using deli ham due to the moisture content. There's no need to thaw the crust before assembling. However, we do recommend using a traditional 9-inch pie shell and not a deep-dish.

Macadamia-Mango Chicken

prep: 15 min. • **cook: 10 min.** • **other: 1 hr.**

The taste of mango is a cross between a pineapple and a peach. It adds a Caribbean-style flavor to this grilled dish.

½ cup soy sauce
2 garlic cloves, minced
1 Tbsp. brown sugar
1 Tbsp. olive oil
1 tsp. grated fresh ginger
6 skinned and boned chicken breasts
3 Tbsp. macadamia nuts, chopped
Mango Salsa

1. Combine first 5 ingredients in a shallow dish or a zip-top plastic freezer bag; add chicken. Cover or seal, and chill 1 hour, turning once.
2. Preheat gril to 350° to 400° (medium-high). Remove chicken from marinade, and discard marinade.
3. Grill, covered with lid, over medium-high heat (350° to 400°) 5 to 6 minutes on each side or until done. Sprinkle evenly with nuts. Serve with Mango Salsa. **Yield:** 6 servings.

mango salsa

prep: 15 min.

1 mango, peeled and chopped*
⅓ cup diced red onion
⅓ cup chopped fresh cilantro
1 Tbsp. fresh lime juice

1. Stir together all ingredients. Cover and chill until ready to serve. **Yield:** about 1½ cups.

*1½ cups chopped jarred refrigerated mango may be substituted.

Pineapple Salsa: Substitute 2 cups chopped fresh pineapple for mango, and reduce red onion and cilantro to 2 Tbsp. Omit lime juice. Stir together pineapple, onion, and cilantro. Whisk together ¼ cup orange juice, 2 Tbsp. lemon juice, 1 Tbsp. honey, ¼ tsp. salt, and ¼ tsp. ground pepper. Stir pineapple mixture into orange juice mixture. Cover and chill 2 hours.

Tasty Turkey Burgers With Herb-Grilled Vidalia Onion Rings

prep: 15 min. • **cook:** 12 min.

1 lb. ground turkey
⅓ cup Italian-seasoned breadcrumbs
1 large egg, beaten
¼ cup finely chopped green bell pepper
1 Tbsp. minced dried onion
½ tsp. salt
½ tsp. freshly ground pepper
4 hamburger buns
Herb-Grilled Vidalia Onion Rings

1. Preheat grill to 350° to 400° (medium-high). Combine first 7 ingredients. Shape mixture into 4 equal-size patties.

2. Grill, covered with grill lid, over medium-high heat (350° to 400°) 5 to 6 minutes on each side or until no longer pink in center.

3. Grill buns, cut sides down, 2 minutes or until toasted. Serve burgers on buns with Herb-Grilled Onion Rings and desired toppings. **Yield:** 4 servings.

Classic Burgers: Substitute 1 lb. ground chuck for ground turkey. Prepare recipe as directed.

Sweet and juicy Vidalia onions are one of summer's greatest Southern treasures. To be classified as a Vidalia onion, it has to be harvested in one of 20 counties to which Georgia's state legislature grants legal permission for production.

herb-grilled vidalia onion rings

prep: 15 min. • **cook:** 8 min.

¼ cup vegetable oil
2 Tbsp. balsamic vinegar
1½ Tbsp. chopped fresh cilantro
1 Tbsp. chopped fresh rosemary
½ tsp. kosher salt
Freshly ground pepper to taste
2 large Vidalia onions

1. Preheat grill to 350° to 400° (medium-high). Stir together first 5 ingredients in a small bowl. Season with pepper to taste.

2. Cut each onion into ½-inch-thick slices. Brush slices evenly with 2½ Tbsp. herb marinade.

3. Grill, covered with grill lid, over medium-high heat (350° to 400°) 4 to 6 minutes on each side or until tender, basting once with remaining marinade. **Yield:** 4 servings.

Pan-Seared Trout With Italian-Style Salsa

prep: 5 min. • cook: 2 min. per batch

6   (6-oz.) trout fillets
¾   tsp. salt
½   tsp. freshly ground pepper
4   Tbsp. olive oil, divided
Italian-Style Salsa
Garnish: lemon slices

1. Sprinkle fillets with salt and pepper.
2. Cook 3 fillets in 2 Tbsp. hot oil in a large nonstick skillet over medium high heat 1 to 2 minutes on each side or until fish flakes with a fork. Repeat with remaining fillets and oil. Top fish with salsa. Garnish, if desired, and serve immediately. **Yield:** 6 servings.

italian-style salsa

prep: 10 min.

4   plum tomatoes, chopped
½   small red onion, finely
    chopped
12 kalamata olives, pitted and
    chopped
2   garlic cloves, minced
2   Tbsp. chopped fresh parsley
1   Tbsp. balsamic vinegar
1   Tbsp. olive oil
2   tsp. drained capers
¼   tsp. salt
¼   tsp. freshly ground pepper
¼   cup crumbled feta cheese
    (optional)

1. Stir together first 10 ingredients, and, if desired, feta cheese, in a medium bowl. Cover and chill until ready to serve. **Yield:** 2 cups.

Blueberry Soup

prep: 10 min. • cook: 10 min. • other: 4 hr., 5 min.

4½ cups fresh blueberries*
1   (12-oz.) can frozen lemonade
     concentrate, thawed
½   cup cold water
1   tsp. dried lavender
1   tsp. vanilla extract
1½ cups vanilla yogurt
Sweet Treat Croutons

1. Stir together fresh blueberries, lemonade concentrate, and ½ cup cold water in a 3-qt. saucepan. Bring to a boil; reduce heat, stir in dried lavender, and simmer, stirring occasionally, 5 minutes or until blueberries burst. Remove from heat, and cool 5 minutes. Stir in vanilla extract.
2. Press mixture through a fine wire-mesh strainer into a large bowl, using back of a spoon to squeeze out juice. Discard pulp. Stir in yogurt. Cover and chill 4 to 24 hours. Serve with Sweet Treat Croutons. **Yield:** 4 to 5 servings.

*2 (12-oz.) packages frozen blueberries may be substituted.

Dress up this cool and colorful soup with a garnish of Sweet Treat Croutons, made from pound cake, or a sprig of fresh lavender. You can make toasty crouton bites with homemade pound cake too. They're also a grand addition to fondue, your favorite ice cream, or as a topping on fresh fruit salad.

sweet treat croutons

prep: 10 min. • cook: 10 min. • other: 30 min.

½   (10.75-oz.) package frozen
     butter pound cake, thawed
3   Tbsp. butter, melted
1   Tbsp. chopped fresh mint

1. Preheat oven to 400°. Cut butter pound cake into ½-inch cubes, and place in a large bowl. Add butter and chopped fresh mint, and toss gently to coat.
2. Place cubes in a single layer on a baking sheet.
3. Bake at 400° for 10 minutes or until lightly toasted. Cool completely (about 30 minutes). **Yield:** about 2 cups.

Gazpacho

prep: 40 min. • **other: 8 hrs.**

Boiled shrimp with tails attached make a pretty garnish and a tasty prize that takes on flavors during its short stint in the zesty summer soup.

8   large tomatoes
2   cucumbers, peeled and
    seeded
1   large green bell pepper,
    seeded
1   large yellow bell pepper,
    seeded
1   small red onion
1   jalapeño pepper, seeded
1   large garlic clove
1   (32-oz.) bottle vegetable juice
⅓   cup red wine vinegar
1   Tbsp. lemon zest
¼   cup fresh lemon juice
2   tsp. salt
1   tsp. paprika
2   to 3 tsp. hot sauce
Toppings: sour cream, chopped
    avocado, croutons, boiled
    shrimp, fresh cilantro sprigs
    (optional)

1. Peel tomatoes. Cut tomatoes, cucumbers, bell peppers, and onion into quarters.

2. Process vegetables, jalapeño pepper, and garlic in a food processor, in batches, until chunky, stopping to scrape down sides. Transfer mixture to a large bowl, and stir in vegetable juice and next 6 ingredients. Cover and chill soup, stirring often, 8 hours. Serve with toppings, if desired. **Yield:** 10 to 12 servings.

how to seed a jalapeño pepper

1. Wearing protective gloves, use a paring knife to cut off the stem and slice the pepper in half lengthwise.   2. Cut each half lengthwise to create 4 separate strips.   3. Lay skin side down, and slide the knife against the pepper to cut away the vein and seeds.

Zucchini-Potato Soup

prep: 20 min. • **cook: 31 min.** • **other: 5 min.**

1 medium leek
4 bacon slices
⅓ cup chopped celery
1 garlic clove, minced
4 cups low-sodium fat-free chicken broth
1 lb. zucchini, sliced (about 3 small squash)
½ lb. small new potatoes, quartered
1 cup half-and-half
⅓ cup chopped fresh parsley
¼ tsp. kosher salt
¼ tsp. pepper

1. Remove root, tough outer leaves, and tops from leek, leaving 2 inches of dark leaves. Thinly slice leek; rinse well, and drain.

2. Cook bacon in a large Dutch oven over medium-high heat 8 to 10 minutes or until crisp; remove bacon, and drain on paper towels, reserving 2 Tbsp. drippings in Dutch oven. Crumble bacon.

3. Sauté leek, celery, and garlic in hot drippings 3 to 4 minutes or until tender. Add chicken broth, zucchini, and potatoes, and simmer 20 to 25 minutes. Stir in half-and-half, parsley, salt, and pepper. Remove from heat, and cool 5 minutes.

4. Process potato mixture, in batches, in a blender or food processor until smooth, stopping to scrape down sides as needed. Sprinkle with crumbled bacon, and serve immediately, or if desired, cover and chill 4 to 6 hours. **Yield:** 4 to 5 servings.

Inspired by the classic potato-and-leek vichyssoise, we added zucchini and gave this recipe our Southern twist with the addition of crisp, crumbled bacon. Prepare this soup the day before you want to serve it. Just pour into chilled bowls to serve.

how to cut & clean leaks

1. Trim the feathery root portion just above the base. Slice off the fibrous green tops, leaving only the white-to-light-green stalk. Discard greens. 2. Cut leek in half lengthwise. Slice or chop leek as specified in your recipe. 3. Place cut leek in a colander, and submerge in a bowl of water. Agitate the leek so any dirt falls to the bottom. Drain the leek on paper towels.

Corn-and-Crab Chowder

prep: 20 min. · **cook: 47 min.**

Corn-and-Crab Chowder is worth the splurge to buy fresh crabmeat, but it's just as good with fresh shrimp.

6   bacon slices
2   celery ribs, diced
1   medium-size green bell pepper, diced
1   medium onion, diced
1   jalapeño pepper, seeded and diced
1   (32-oz.) container chicken broth
3   Tbsp. all-purpose flour
3   cups fresh corn kernels (6 ears)
1   lb. fresh lump crabmeat, drained and picked*
1   cup whipping cream
¼   cup chopped fresh cilantro
½   tsp. salt
¼   tsp. pepper
Oyster crackers
Garnish: chopped fresh cilantro

1. Cook bacon in a Dutch oven over medium heat 8 to 10 minutes or until crisp; remove bacon, and drain on paper towels, reserving 2 Tbsp. drippings in Dutch oven. Crumble bacon.
2. Sauté celery and next 3 ingredients in hot drippings 5 to 6 minutes or until tender.
3. Whisk together broth and flour until smooth. Add to celery mixture. Stir in corn. Bring to a boil; reduce heat, and simmer, stirring occasionally, 30 minutes. Gently stir in crabmeat and next 4 ingredients; cook 4 to 5 minutes or until thoroughly heated. Serve warm with crumbled bacon and oyster crackers. Garnish, if desired. **Yield:** 6 to 8 servings.

*1 lb. peeled cooked shrimp or chopped cooked chicken may be substituted.

tips from our kitchen

Freezer Ready To freeze this soup, select heavy-duty freezer containers to pack and store it. Fill the container to the recommended capacity to preserve the soup's freshness. Chill the soup completely in the refrigerator before freezing, but be sure to cool it first. You can quickly chill it by placing frozen water bottles directly in the soup. If you choose not to freeze Corn-and-Crab Chowder, you can store it in an airtight container in the coldest part of your refrigerator for up to 24 hours.

Frogmore Stew

Frogmore Stew

prep: 10 min. · **cook:** 23 min.

¼ cup Old Bay Seasoning
4 lb. small red potatoes
2 lb. kielbasa or hot smoked
  link sausage, cut into
  1½-inch pieces
6 ears fresh corn, halved
4 lb. unpeeled, large fresh
  shrimp
Old Bay Seasoning
Cocktail sauce

1. Bring 5 qt. water and ¼ cup Old Bay Seasoning to a rolling boil in a large covered stockpot.
2. Add potatoes; return to a boil, and cook, uncovered, 10 minutes.
3. Add sausage and corn, and return to a boil. Cook 10 minutes or until potatoes are tender.
4. Add shrimp to stockpot; cook 3 to 4 minutes or until shrimp turn pink. Drain. Serve with Old Bay Seasoning and cocktail sauce. **Yield:** 12 servings.

note: For testing purposes only, we used Hillshire Farm Kielbasa.

Smoky Speckled Butterbeans

prep: 10 min. · **cook:** 3 hr.

1 lb. smoked pork shoulder
2 lb. fresh or frozen speckled
  butterbeans
2 tsp. salt
1 tsp. pepper
1 jalapeño pepper, sliced
Hot cooked rice (optional)
Toppings: chowchow, chopped
  sweet onion, or hot sauce
  (optional)

1. Bring 3 qt. water and first 5 ingredients to a boil in a Dutch oven. Reduce heat to medium. Cover and simmer 3 hours or until beans are tender, stirring occasionally. Remove pork and shred. Return to Dutch oven. Serve with rice and toppings, if desired. **Yield:** 8 servings.

Crowder Pea Succotash

prep: 20 min. • cook: 8 min.

Crowder peas are also known as cowpeas. The hulls can be any color from white to purple to black.

¼ large onion, finely diced
1 green bell pepper, finely diced
1 red bell pepper, finely diced
3 Tbsp. olive oil
2 cups fresh or frozen corn kernels
Crowder Peas
½ cup reserved Crowder Peas liquid
½ cup sliced green onions
1 Tbsp. fresh thyme leaves, finely chopped
½ tsp. salt
Garnish: fresh thyme sprig

1. Sauté onion and bell peppers in hot oil in a large skillet over medium heat 5 to 7 minutes or until tender. Stir in corn and Crowder Peas; cook 2 minutes or until thoroughly heated. Stir in ½ cup reserved Crowder Peas liquid, green onions, thyme, and salt; cook 1 to 2 minutes or until thoroughly heated. Garnish, if desired. Serve immediately. **Yield:** 8 servings.

crowder peas

prep: 15 min. • cook: 25 min. • other: 30 min.

½ large onion, cut in half
½ medium carrot, cut in half lengthwise
2 celery ribs, cut into 2-inch pieces
2 garlic cloves, peeled and cut in half
1 Tbsp. olive oil
2 Tbsp. jarred ham base
2 cups fresh or frozen crowder peas
2 fresh thyme sprigs
½ tsp. salt
½ tsp. pepper

1. Cook first 4 ingredients in hot oil in a Dutch oven over medium-high heat, stirring often, 5 minutes. Stir in ham base and 4 cups of water until well blended. Add peas, thyme, salt, and pepper, and bring mixture to a boil. Reduce heat to low, and simmer 20 minutes or until peas are done. Remove from heat; cool 30 minutes.
2. Drain peas, reserving cooking liquid for another use. Remove and discard onion, carrots, celery, and thyme sprigs. **Yield:** 4 servings.

note: For testing purposes only, we used Superior Touch Better Than Bouillon ham base.

Fresh Corn Cakes

Fresh Corn Cakes

prep: 20 min. • **cook:** 5 min. per batch

2½ cups fresh corn kernels
   (about 5 ears)
3 large eggs
¾ cup milk
3 Tbsp. butter, melted
¾ cup all-purpose flour
¾ cup yellow or white cornmeal
1 (8-oz.) package fresh
   mozzarella cheese, grated
2 Tbsp. chopped fresh chives
1 tsp. salt
1 tsp. freshly ground pepper

1. Pulse first 4 ingredients together in a food processor 3 to 4 times or just until corn is coarsely chopped.
2. Stir together flour and next 5 ingredients in a large bowl; stir in corn mixture just until dry ingredients are moistened.
3. Spoon ⅛ cup batter for each cake onto a hot, lightly greased griddle or large nonstick skillet to form 2-inch cakes (do not spread or flatten cakes). Cook cakes 3 to 4 minutes or until tops are covered with bubbles and edges look cooked. Turn and cook other sides 2 to 3 minutes. **Yield:** about 3 dozen.

Skillet Creamed Corn

prep: 20 min. • **cook:** 20 min.

6 bacon slices
½ Vidalia onion, finely chopped
1 garlic clove, finely chopped
3 cups fresh corn kernels
   (about 6 ears)
¼ cup all-purpose flour
1½ cups half-and-half
½ tsp. salt
¼ tsp. pepper
1 Tbsp. butter
1 Tbsp. chopped fresh basil
Garnish: fresh basil sprigs

1. Cook bacon in a large skillet until crisp; remove bacon, and drain on paper towels, reserving 2 Tbsp. drippings in skillet. Crumble bacon, and set aside.
2. Sauté onion and garlic in hot drippings 5 minutes or until tender. Stir in corn; cook 5 to 7 minutes or until golden. Remove from heat.
3. Cook flour in a large clean skillet over medium heat, stirring occasionally, about 5 minutes or until golden. Gradually whisk in half-and-half until smooth. Add corn mixture, salt, and pepper; cook 5 minutes or until thickened. Remove from heat; stir in butter and basil. Sprinkle each serving with bacon, and garnish, if desired. **Yield:** 6 servings.

Eggplant-Squash-Tomato Sauté

prep: 20 min.   •   cook: 20 min.

Fresh, bright, and healthy, this richly colored side is loaded with nutrients.

1   medium onion, chopped
1   Tbsp. olive oil
1   lb. eggplant, peeled and cubed
1   lb. yellow squash, chopped
1   lb. plum tomatoes, chopped
1   Tbsp. fresh oregano, chopped
1   tsp. salt
½   tsp. minced garlic
¼   tsp. ground red pepper

1. Sauté onion in hot oil in a large nonstick skillet over medium-high heat 5 minutes or until crisp-tender. Add eggplant and squash. Cover and cook, stirring occasionally, 10 minutes or until eggplant begins to soften. Stir in tomatoes and remaining ingredients. Cover and cook 5 more minutes. **Yield:** 8 servings.

how to peel and mince garlic

1. To loosen the papery skin, place the flat side of a chef's kitchen knife on an unpeeled clove. To crush, press down using the heel of your hand. Peel off the skin. Remove the tough end with a knife.   2. To mince, make lengthwise cuts through the clove; cut the strips crosswise for chopped or minced pieces.   3. Using a garlic press is another method to mince or crush garlic. Place a peeled clove in the press; force it through the tiny holes.

Cajun Green Bean Stir-fry

prep: 10 min. • cook: 11 min.

2 lb. fresh green beans, trimmed and cut into 2-inch pieces
2 tsp. minced garlic
2 Tbsp. olive oil
¾ cup oven-roasted-flavored sliced almonds
1¼ tsp. Cajun seasoning, divided

1. Bring beans and salted water to cover to a boil in a Dutch oven. Boil 7 minutes or until crisp-tender; drain. Plunge into ice water to stop the cooking process; drain. Wipe Dutch oven clean with paper towels.
2. Cook garlic in hot oil in Dutch oven over medium heat 1 minute; add beans, and sauté 2 minutes. Add almonds and ¾ tsp. Cajun seasoning; sauté 1 minute.
3. Place beans in a serving dish, and sprinkle with remaining ½ tsp. Cajun seasoning. **Yield:** 6 servings.

note: For testing purposes only, we used Sunkist Almond Accents Original Oven Roasted Flavored Sliced Almonds.

This savory side dish cooks up quick, and the Cajun seasoning gives it a distinctive flavor making it a perfect choice for a dinner with friends.

Green Bean, Grape, and Pasta Toss

prep: 25 min. • cook: 15 min. • other: 3 hr.

1 cup chopped pecans
8 bacon slices
1 lb. thin fresh green beans, trimmed and cut in half
1 (8-oz.) package penne pasta
1 cup mayonnaise
⅓ cup sugar
⅓ cup red wine vinegar
1 tsp. salt
2 cups seedless red grapes, cut in half
⅓ cup diced red onion
Salt to taste

1. Preheat oven to 350°. Arrange pecans in a single layer on a baking sheet, and bake at 350° for 5 to 7 minutes or until lightly toasted and fragrant.
2. Cook bacon in a large skillet over medium-high heat 5 to 7 minutes or until crisp; remove bacon, and drain on paper towels. Crumble bacon.
3. Cook beans in boiling salted water to cover 5 minutes or until crisp-tender; drain. Plunge beans into ice water to stop the cooking process.
4. Meanwhile, prepare pasta according to package directions; drain.
5. Whisk together mayonnaise and next 3 ingredients in a large bowl; add pecans, green beans, pasta, grapes, and onion, stirring to coat. Season with salt to taste. Cover and chill 3 hours; stir in bacon just before serving. **Yield:** 8 servings.

Peppery Grilled Okra With Lemon-Basil Dipping Sauce

prep: 15 min. • cook: 4 min. • other: 24 hr., 5 min.

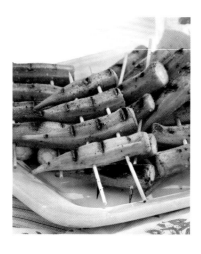

Cheesecloth or coffee filter
1   (32-oz.) container plain
    low-fat yogurt
¼   cup chopped fresh basil
2   Tbsp. lemon juice
½   tsp. minced garlic
¼   tsp. sugar
1½ tsp. salt, divided
1¼ tsp. freshly ground pepper,
    divided
2   lb. fresh okra, trimmed
2   Tbsp. olive oil
Garnish: freshly ground pepper

1. Line a wire-mesh strainer with 3 layers of cheese-cloth or 1 (12-cup) coffee filter. Place strainer over a bowl. Spoon yogurt into strainer. Cover and chill 24 hours. Remove yogurt, discarding strained liquid.
2. Preheat grill to 400° to 450° (high) heat. Combine strained yogurt, basil, next 3 ingredients, ½ tsp. salt, and ¼ tsp. pepper. Cover and chill until ready to serve.
3. Toss together okra, olive oil, and remaining 1 tsp. salt and 1 tsp. pepper in a large bowl.
4. Grill okra, covered with grill lid, over 400° to 450° (high) heat 2 to 3 minutes on each side or until tender. Cool 5 minutes.
5. Transfer okra to a serving dish, and serve with dipping sauce. Garnish, if desired. **Yield:** 8 servings.

Fried Okra and Green Tomatoes

prep: 18 min. • cook: 6 min. per batch

1   cup buttermilk
1   large egg
1¾ cups cornmeal
¾   tsp. salt, divided
¼   tsp. pepper
1   lb. fresh okra, sliced
2   green tomatoes, cut into
    ½-inch pieces
Vegetable oil

1. Whisk together buttermilk and egg.
2. Combine cornmeal, ¼ tsp. salt, and pepper. Dip okra and tomato, in batches, into buttermilk mixture; coat in cornmeal mixture.
3. Pour oil to a depth of 2 inches into a Dutch oven. Heat oil to 375°.
4. Fry okra and tomatoes, in batches, 6 minutes turning once, or until golden. (Turning too soon will cause breading to fall off.) Drain on paper towels; sprinkle with remaining ½ tsp. salt. **Yield:** 8 servings.

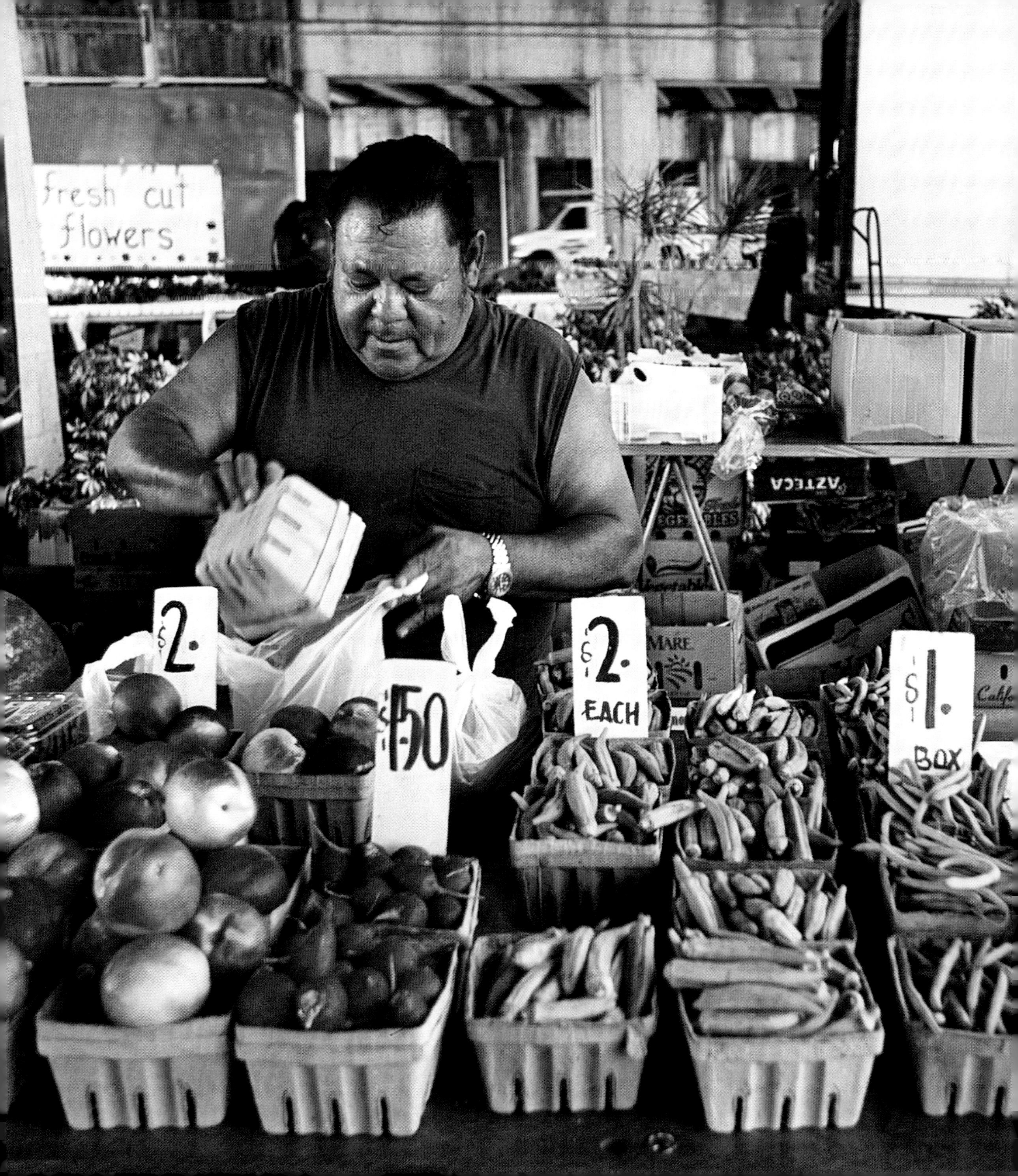

fresh cut
flowers

$2.

$1.50

$2.
EACH

$1.
BOX

Kamala Gamble, Chef & Gardener

Guilford Gardens, Oklahoma City, Oklahoma

Kamala Gamble talks faster than an auctioneer, but when it comes to food, this trained chef and organic gardener wants the world to slow down. The cofounder of Slow Food Oklahoma City, Kamala believes that meals made from naturally produced local vegetables, fruits, meats, and dairy products are good for your health, good for the local economy, and good for your taste buds.

"Slow food" is a worldwide movement dedicated to promoting local artisans who grow, market, prepare, and serve wholesome and fresh traditional foods. Kamala (rhymes with "Pamela") bought into the movement while cooking at Chicago's famed Frontera Grill, where nearly every ingredient is locally produced. When she moved back to Oklahoma in 2001 and bought a house with a big backyard, the next step seemed obvious. "I said, 'Oh, I'll just start a garden.'" Her soil, unfortunately, was "horrid, black clay."

After 8 years of hard work and upkeep, today, the 1½-acre plot, called Guilford Gardens, is a highly productive Community Supported Agriculture (CSA) farm that sells organic produce to approximately 80 local subscribers. Each week for 8 to 12 weeks, subscribers pick up a basket of vegetables of varying contents. Kamala grows more than 15 kinds of tomatoes, 20 kinds of peppers, 4 varieties of potatoes, 4 kinds of onions, and 6 kinds of eggplant. With so many fresh food options, the possibilities for healthy eating are practically endless.

Rustic Vidalia Onion Tart

prep: 15 min. • **cook:** 25 min. • **other:** 5 min.

2   Tbsp. butter
4   medium-size Vidalia onions,
    thinly sliced (about 6¼ cups)
1½ tsp. chopped fresh rosemary
¾   tsp. salt
½   tsp. pepper
½   (15-oz.) package refrigerated
    piecrusts
Parchment paper
1   egg white, lightly beaten
¾   cup (3 oz.) shredded Gruyère
    cheese, divided

1. Preheat oven to 425°. Melt butter in a large non-stick skillet over medium-high heat; add onion and next 3 ingredients. Cook, stirring occasionally, 8 minutes or until tender.
2. Unroll piecrust onto a lightly floured surface. Pat or roll into a 12-inch circle. Place piecrust on a parchment paper-lined baking sheet. Brush with egg white. Sprinkle ½ cup cheese in center of crust. Spoon onion mixture over cheese, leaving a 2½-inch border. Sprinkle remaining ¼ cup cheese over onion. Fold piecrust border up and over onion, pleating as you go and leaving a 4-inch-wide opening in center. Brush crust with egg white.
3. Bake at 425° on bottom oven rack 17 to 19 minutes or until crust is golden. Let stand 5 minutes before serving. **Yield:** 6 servings.

Don't worry about being exact when folding the piecrust. It's meant to look organic and free-form, allowing the filling to show through.

Summer Squash Casserole

prep: 25 min. • **cook: 35 min.** • **other: 10 min.**

The addition of water chestnuts adds a flavorful crunch to this casserole.

1½ lb. yellow squash
1 lb. zucchini
1 small sweet onion, chopped
2½ tsp. salt, divided
1 cup grated carrots
1 (10¾-oz.) can cream of chicken soup
1 (8-oz.) container sour cream
1 (8-oz.) can water chestnuts, drained and chopped
1 (8-oz.) bag herb-seasoned stuffing
½ cup butter, melted

1. Preheat oven to 350°. Cut squash and zucchini into ¼-inch-thick slices; place in a Dutch oven. Add chopped onion, 2 tsp. salt, and water to cover. Bring to a boil over medium-high heat, and cook 5 minutes; drain well.

2. Stir together grated carrots, next 3 ingredients, and remaining ½ tsp. salt in a large bowl; fold in squash mixture. Stir together stuffing and melted butter; spoon half of stuffing mixture into bottom of a lightly greased 13- x 9-inch baking dish. Spoon squash mixture over stuffing mixture, and top with remaining stuffing mixture.

3. Bake at 350° for 30 to 35 minutes or until bubbly and golden brown, shielding with aluminum foil after 20 to 25 minutes to prevent excessive browning. Let stand 10 minutes before serving. **Yield:** 8 servings.

note: For testing purposes only, we used Pepperidge Farm Herb Seasoned Stuffing.

tips from the farm

Squash Notes Squash are members of the gourd family and are generally divided into two categories—summer squash and winter squash. Crookneck (yellow) squash and zucchini squash (similar in appearance to cucumbers) are two of the most common summer squash. At their peak during summer months, they are best eaten while young and tender. Their flesh has a high water content and mild flavor that doesn't require long cooking. Store squash in a perforated plastic bag in the refrigerator crisper drawer for up to 3 days. The skin and seeds are edible, so you don't have to worry about peeling and seeding them.

Tomato-Zucchini Tart

prep: 20 min. • cook: 21 min.

½ (15-oz.) package refrigerated piecrusts
1 medium zucchini, thinly sliced (about ¾ lb.)
2 tsp. olive oil
3 medium plum tomatoes, sliced
½ cup fresh basil, chopped
⅓ cup (1½ oz.) freshly grated Parmesan cheese
⅓ cup light mayonnaise
½ tsp. freshly ground pepper

1. Preheat oven to 450°. Fit piecrust into a 9-inch tart pan according to package directions; trim excess. Prick bottom and sides of piecrust using a fork.
2. Bake piecrust at 450° for 9 to 11 minutes or until lightly browned. Remove from oven, and let cool.
3. Reduce oven temperature to 425°. Sauté zucchini in hot oil in a large skillet over medium-high heat 2 minutes or until tender. Arrange zucchini in bottom of prepared piecrust. Arrange tomatoes on top of zucchini.
4. Stir together basil, cheese, and mayonnaise. Drop by teaspoonfuls evenly on top of tomatoes, and spread gently. Sprinkle with pepper.
5. Bake at 425° for 10 to 15 minutes or until thoroughly heated and cheese mixture is slightly melted. **Yield:** 8 servings.

Make quick work of slicing or chopping fresh basil by rolling up a small bunch of leaves and snipping it into shreds. To chop it, snip the shreds crosswise.

tips from our kitchen

Storing Basil After buying fresh basil, wrap the stems in a damp paper towel then in plastic wrap. Place the bundle in the door of your refrigerator where it is not as cold. The basil will generally keep up to 1 week.

Balsamic Grilled Veggies

prep: 20 min. • **cook: 20 min.**

Grilling adds a new level of tastiness to fresh vegetables.

2   Tbsp. olive oil
1   Tbsp. dried or ¼ cup chopped
    fresh basil
1   Tbsp. balsamic vinegar
2   tsp. kosher or 1½ tsp. table
    salt
1   tsp. pepper
1   fennel bulb
1   large red onion, cut into
    1-inch pieces
1   (8-oz.) package fresh
    mushrooms
1   pt. cherry tomatoes
2   medium zucchini, cut into
    1-inch pieces
4   small yellow squash, cut into
    1-inch pieces

1. Preheat grill to 350° to 400° (medium-high) heat. Stir together olive oil and next 4 ingredients in a small bowl.

2. Rinse fennel thoroughly. Trim and discard root end of fennel bulb. Trim stalks from bulb, reserving fronds for another use. Cut bulb in half vertically, and remove core. Cut bulb into ½-inch-thick slices.

3. Toss fennel, onion, and mushrooms with half of olive oil mixture, and place in a grill wok or metal basket.

4. Grill, covered with grill lid, 10 minutes over 350° to 400° (medium-high) heat. Toss tomatoes, zucchini, and yellow squash with remaining olive oil mixture. Add to grill wok or basket. Grill, covered with grill lid, stirring occasionally, 10 to 15 minutes or until vegetables are tender. Serve immediately. **Yield:** 6 servings.

how to chop an onion

1. Halve a peeled onion through the root end. Place cut side down on a cutting board. Make several horizontal cuts parallel to the board, cutting close to but not through the root end. 2. Make lengthwise vertical cuts, to but not through the root. 3. Cut across the onion to chop it into even pieces, sized according to recipe directions.

Angela's Vegetable Frittata

prep: 15 min. • **cook: 29 min.**

2   large leeks
2   Tbsp. olive oil, divided
1   cup diced cooked potato
1   lb. summer squash, sliced
2   Tbsp. chopped fresh parsley
½   tsp. chopped fresh thyme
½   tsp. freshly ground pepper
¾   tsp. salt, divided
8   large eggs
½   cup milk
¾   cup (3 oz.) shredded
    Parmesan cheese, divided

1. Preheat oven to 450°. Remove and discard root ends and dark green tops of leeks. Cut in half lengthwise, and rinse thoroughly under cold running water to remove grit and sand. Thinly slice leeks.

2. Sauté leeks in 1 Tbsp. hot oil in a 10-inch ovenproof skillet over medium-high heat 4 to 5 minutes or until tender. Remove from skillet. Sauté potato in remaining 1 Tbsp. oil in skillet 3 to 4 minutes or until golden. Add squash, and sauté 10 minutes. Stir in leeks, parsley, thyme, pepper, and ½ tsp. salt until blended.

3. Process eggs, milk, ½ cup Parmesan cheese, ¼ cup water and remaining ¼ tsp. salt in a blender until blended; pour over leek mixture in skillet. Cook over medium heat, without stirring, 2 minutes or until edges of frittata are set. (Edges should appear firm when pan is gently shaken; the top layer should appear wet.) Sprinkle with remaining ¼ cup cheese.

4. Bake at 450° for 10 to 12 minutes or until center is set. **Yield:** 6 to 8 servings.

To preserve the herbs' freshness, store them, stems down, in a glass of water with a plastic bag over the leaves in the refrigerator. Change the water every other day.

**Double Berry
Freezer Jam**

Double Berry Freezer Jam

prep: 10 min. • **other: 20 min.**

4   cups fresh whole blueberries
3   cups fresh strawberries
1½ cups sugar
1   (1.59-oz.) envelope freezer
    jam pectin

1. Pulse blueberries in food processor 2 to 4 times or until finely chopped, stopping to scrape down sides. Place in a medium-size bowl. Pulse strawberries in food processor 8 to 10 times or until finely chopped, stopping to scrape down sides. Add to blueberries in bowl. Stir in sugar, and let stand 15 minutes.
2. Gradually stir in pectin. Stir for 3 minutes; let stand 5 minutes.
3. Spoon mixture into sterilized canning jars, filling to ½ inch from top; wipe jar rims clean. Cover with metal lids, and screw on bands. Place in freezer. **Yield:** about 5 cups.

Pair this jam with some peanut butter for a mighty fine sandwich.

Granny Smith Apple Freezer Jam

prep: 15 min. • **other: 20 min.**

5   cups coarsely chopped,
    unpeeled Granny Smith
    apples (about 5 medium
    apples or 1½ lb.)
1   cup sugar
½   cup pasteurized apple juice
1   (1.59-oz.) envelope freezer
    jam pectin

1. Pulse chopped apples in food processor 10 times or until finely chopped. Place in a medium bowl. Stir in sugar and juice; let stand 15 minutes.
2. Gradually stir in pectin. Stir for 3 minutes; let stand 5 minutes.
3. Spoon fruit mixture into sterilized canning jars, filling to ½ inch from top; wipe jar rims clean. Cover with metal lids, and screw on bands. Place in freezer. **Yield:** about 3½ cups.

Peach-Rosemary Jam

prep: 25 min. • cook: 2 min. • other: 10 min.

Decorative jars make pretty serving containers, but be sure to use jars made specifically for preserving foods when processing canned items.

4 cups peeled and chopped fresh peaches or nectarines
1 tsp. lime zest
¼ cup fresh lime juice
2 rosemary sprigs
1 (1.75-oz.) package powdered fruit pectin
5 cups sugar

1. Bring first 5 ingredients to a full rolling boil in a Dutch oven. Boil 1 minute, stirring constantly. Add sugar to peach mixture, and bring to a full rolling boil; boil 1 minute, stirring constantly. Remove from heat. Remove and discard rosemary sprigs; skim off foam with a metal spoon.

2. Pour hot mixture immediately into hot, sterilized jars, filling to ¼ inch from top. Remove air bubbles; wipe jar rims. Cover at once with metal lids, and screw on bands.

3. Process jars in boiling-water bath 10 minutes.
Yield: 7 (½-pint) jars.

Fig Preserves

prep: 10 min. • cook: 2 hr. • other: 8 hr., 15 min.

2 qt. fresh figs (about 4 lb.)
8 cups sugar

1. Layer figs and sugar in a Dutch oven. Cover and let stand 8 hours.
2. Cook over medium heat 2 hours, stirring occasionally, until syrup thickens and figs are clear.
3. Pack figs into hot, sterilized jars, filling to ½ inch from top. Cover fruit with boiling syrup, filling to ½ inch from top. Remove air bubbles; wipe jar rims. Cover at once with metal lids, and screw on bands.
4. Process jars in boiling-water bath 15 minutes.
Yield: 4 qt.

Mango Chutney

prep: 30 min. • cook: 30 min.

1½ cups orange juice
1 cup golden raisins
3 cups chopped mango (about 2 medium)
2 to 3 jalapeño peppers, seeded and chopped
1 medium-size red onion, chopped
2 Tbsp. brown sugar
2 to 3 Tbsp. lime juice
2 tsp. ground coriander
1 tsp. ground cumin
1 tsp. ground ginger
¼ tsp. ground cloves
¼ tsp. ground nutmeg
⅛ tsp. ground red pepper

1. Combine all ingredients in a medium saucepan. Cover mixture, and bring to a boil over medium heat, stirring occasionally. Reduce heat, and simmer, uncovered, 30 minutes or until mixture thickens, stirring occasionally. Cool slightly. Chill up to 1 week.
Yield: 2 cups.

Grilled Peach-and-Mozzarella Salad

prep: 25 min. • **cook: 6 min.**

5   peaches (not white)
3   green onions, sliced
¼   cup chopped fresh cilantro
3   Tbsp. honey
1   tsp. salt
1   tsp. lime zest
½   cup fresh lime juice
¾   tsp. ground cumin
¾   tsp. chili powder
1½ Tbsp. tequila (optional)
⅓   cup olive oil
Vegetable cooking spray
1   (6-oz.) package watercress
       or baby arugula, thoroughly
       washed
¾   lb. fresh mozzarella, cut into
       16 (¼-inch) slices
Garnish: fresh cilantro sprigs

1. Peel and chop 1 peach. Cut remaining 4 peaches into 28 (¼-inch-thick) rounds, cutting through stem and bottom ends. (Cut peaches inward from sides, cutting each side just until you reach the pit. Discard pits.)

2. Process chopped peach, green onions, next 7 ingredients, and, if desired, tequila in a food processor 10 to 15 seconds or until smooth. Add oil, and pulse 3 to 4 times or until thoroughly combined.

3. Coat cold cooking grate of grill with cooking spray; place on grill. Preheat grill to 350° to 400° (medium-high). Brush both sides of peach rounds with ⅓ cup peach dressing.

4. Grill peach rounds, covered with grill lid, over 350° to 400° (medium-high) heat 3 to 5 minutes on each side or until grill marks appear.

5. Arrange watercress evenly on 4 plates. Alternately layer 4 grilled peach rounds and 4 cheese slices over watercress on each plate. Top each with 3 more peach rounds. Drizzle with remaining peach dressing. Garnish, if desired. **Yield:** 4 servings.

Grilled Peach-and-Feta Salad: Preheat oven to 350°. Arrange ¼ cup pecans, chopped, in a single layer in a shallow pan. Bake 8 to 10 minutes or until pecans are toasted and fragrant, stirring after 5 minutes. Reduce peaches from 5 to 4, and reduce salt to ½ tsp. Substitute 8 cups loosely packed Bibb lettuce leaves (1 to 2 heads of lettuce) for watercress and ¼ cup crumbled feta cheese for mozzarella. Peel and chop 1 peach. Cut each of remaining 3 peaches into 8 wedges. Proceed with recipe as directed in Steps 2 through 4, decreasing grilling time for peach wedges to 2 to 3 minutes on each side or until grill marks appear. Divide lettuce and 4 cooked bacon slices, halved crosswise, among 4 plates. Top with grilled peach wedges. Sprinkle with feta cheese and pecans. Serve with dressing.

Traditional peaches work better on this dish than white peaches, which have more sugar and water and don't hold up as well on the grill.

Watermelon, Mâche, and Pecan Salad

prep: 20 min. • cook: 5 min. • other: 15 min.

Mâche, a tender heirloom variety of lamb's lettuce, has a slightly sweet, nutty flavor, but the salad is equally good prepared with baby lettuces.

¾ cup chopped pecans
5   cups seeded and cubed
     watermelon
1   (6-oz.) package mâche,
     thoroughly washed
Pepper Jelly Vinaigrette
1   cup crumbled Gorgonzola
     cheese

1. Preheat oven to 350°. Arrange pecans in a single layer on a baking sheet, and bake at 350° for 5 to 7 minutes or until lightly toasted and fragrant. Cool on a wire rack 15 minutes or until completely cool.
2. Combine watermelon and mâche in a large bowl; add vinaigrette, tossing gently to coat. Transfer watermelon mixture to a serving platter, and sprinkle evenly with pecans and cheese. **Yield:** 6 to 8 servings.

pepper jelly vinaigrette

prep: 10 min.

¼ cup rice wine vinegar
¼ cup pepper jelly
1   Tbsp. fresh lime juice
1   Tbsp. grated onion
1   tsp. salt
¼ tsp. pepper
¼ cup vegetable oil

1. Whisk together first 6 ingredients. Gradually add oil in a slow, steady stream, whisking until blended. **Yield:** ¾ cup.

Bacon–Blue Cheese Salad With White Wine Vinaigrette

prep: 35 min. • **cook: 8 min.** • **other: 30 min.**

2   Tbsp. chopped pecans
2   medium cucumbers, peeled
3   cups mixed baby greens
2   cooked thick-cut bacon slices, halved
⅓   cup shredded or matchstick carrots
¼   cup crumbled blue cheese
Salt and freshly ground pepper to taste
White Wine Vinaigrette

1. Preheat oven to 350°. Place chopped pecans in a single layer in a shallow pan.
2. Bake at 350° for 8 minutes or until lightly toasted, stirring occasionally. Let cool 30 minutes or until completely cool.
3. Using a Y-shaped vegetable peeler, cut cucumbers lengthwise into very thin strips just until seeds are visible. Discard cucumber core.
4. Shape largest cucumber slices into 4 (2½- to 2¾-inch-wide) rings. Wrap evenly with remaining cucumber slices. Stand rings upright on 4 serving plates.
5. Fill each cucumber ring evenly with mixed greens, next 3 ingredients, and toasted pecans. Sprinkle with salt and pepper to taste. Drizzle each salad with 1 Tbsp. White Wine Vinaigrette, and serve with remaining vinaigrette. **Yield:** 4 servings.

Serving this salad in cucumber rings makes it suitable for the most special occasions.

white wine vinaigrette

prep: 5 min.

¼   cup white wine vinegar
1   Tbsp. Dijon mustard
1   garlic clove, minced
1   tsp. sugar
½   cup olive oil
Salt and freshly ground pepper to taste

1. Whisk together first 4 ingredients until blended. Add oil in a slow, steady stream, whisking constantly until smooth. Whisk in salt and pepper to taste. Store in the refrigerator in an airtight container up to 1 week. **Yield:** about ⅔ cup.

Green Bean-and-New Potato Salad

prep: 10 min. • **cook: 24 min.**

New potatoes are small, round red-skinned potatoes with a white, waxy flesh that makes them good for boiling. They're called new potatoes because they're harvested while still young.

2 lb. new red potatoes, quartered
1 tsp. salt
2 Tbsp. salt
2 lb. thin fresh green beans, trimmed
Rosemary Vinaigrette

1. Bring new potatoes, 1 tsp. salt, and water to cover to a boil in a Dutch oven; cook 18 to 20 minutes or until potatoes are tender. Drain and let cool.
2. Bring 2 qt. water and 2 Tbsp. salt to a boil in a Dutch oven; add beans. Cook 6 minutes or until crisp-tender; drain. Plunge beans into ice water to stop the cooking process; drain.
3. Combine green beans and potatoes in a large bowl. Pour Rosemary Vinaigrette over green bean mixture, tossing to coat. Cover and chill until ready to serve. **Yield:** 8 servings.

rosemary vinaigrette

prep: 5 min.

½ cup white balsamic vinegar
¼ cup honey
2 garlic cloves
2 Tbsp. chopped fresh rosemary leaves
¼ medium-size red onion
1 Tbsp. Dijon mustard
½ tsp. salt
Freshly ground pepper to taste
½ cup extra virgin olive oil

1. Process balsamic vinegar and next 7 ingredients in a blender or food processor 15 to 20 seconds, stopping to scrape down sides. With blender or processor running, gradually add olive oil in a slow, steady stream; process until smooth. Store dressing in an airtight container in the refrigerator up to 2 days. **Yield:** 1⅓ cups.

Tomato-Cucumber Salad

Tomato-Cucumber Salad

prep: 10 min.

1 seedless cucumber, sliced
½ small onion, thinly sliced
2 cups quartered small,
   vine-ripened tomatoes
¼ cup olive oil-and-vinegar
   dressing
½ tsp. lemon zest
1 Tbsp. lemon juice
Salt and pepper to taste

1. Stir together cucumber, onion, and tomatoes. Add dressing, lemon zest, lemon juice, and salt and pepper. Toss to coat. **Yield:** 4 servings.

note: For testing purposes only, we used Campari tomatoes and Newman's Own Olive Oil & Vinegar Dressing.

You can have this salad on the table 10 minutes after you get home from the market.

Grilled Okra-and-Tomatillo Salad

prep: 15 min. • **cook: 18 min.**

10 fresh tomatillos
Vegetable cooking spray
1 large sweet onion, thinly
   sliced
2 tsp. olive oil, divided
1 lb. fresh okra, trimmed
1 tsp. lime zest
3 Tbsp. fresh lime juice
2 Tbsp. olive oil
1 garlic clove, pressed
¼ cup chopped fresh cilantro
1 tsp. salt
½ tsp. coarsely ground pepper

1. Remove husks from tomatillos; wash thoroughly, and thinly slice.
2. Coat a cold cooking grate with cooking spray; place on grill over medium-high heat (350° to 400°). Place tomatillos on cooking grate, and grill, covered with grill lid, 4 minutes on each side or until tender. Remove from grill; coarsely chop.
3. Toss onion with 1 tsp. olive oil. Grill onion in a grill wok or metal basket, covered with grill lid, over medium-high heat (350° to 400°) 5 minutes or until slightly charred, stirring occasionally. Remove from grill, and coarsely chop.
4. Cut okra in half lengthwise, and toss with remaining 1 tsp. oil. Grill okra in a grill wok or metal basket, covered with grill lid, over medium-high heat (350° to 400°) 5 minutes or until tender, stirring occasionally. Remove from grill.
5. Stir together lime zest and next 6 ingredients in a large bowl; add tomatillos, onion, and okra, tossing to coat. Serve at room temperature. **Yield:** 8 servings.

The tomatillo is often known as a Mexican green tomato. Its distinguishing feature is a paperlike husk, which, if fresh, will be tight-fitting around the fruit. For this recipe, you can substitute 2 large green tomatoes for the tomatillos, if desired.

Succotash Salad

prep: 20 min. • cook: 22 min.

Succotash is an Indian word meaning "broken into bits," referring to its mix of corn kernels and butter beans. Traditionally it was served hot, and sometimes with flecks of red or green bell pepper. Here, it's updated with a chive vinaigrette and served warm or chilled.

1 cup fresh butter beans
2 cups fresh corn kernels (3 large ears)
3 Tbsp. canola oil, divided
2 Tbsp. fresh lemon juice
3 Tbsp. chopped fresh chives
½ tsp. hot sauce
¼ tsp. salt
¼ tsp. pepper

1. Cook butter beans in boiling salted water to cover 20 minutes or until tender; drain.
2. Sauté corn in 1 Tbsp. hot oil in a small skillet over medium-high heat 2 to 3 minutes or until crisp-tender.
3. Whisk together lemon juice, next 4 ingredients, and remaining 2 Tbsp. oil in a large bowl; stir in corn and butter beans. Serve immediately, or cover and chill up to 3 days. **Yield:** 6 servings.

note: For a pretty presentation, serve Succotash Salad stuffed inside hollowed-out tomatoes.

Mustard-Dill Tortellini Salad Skewers

prep: 25 min. • **cook: 2 min.** • **other: 4 hr., 2 min.**

1 (9-oz.) package refrigerated cheese tortellini
1 (8-oz.) package frozen sugar snap peas
68 (4-inch) wooden skewers
1 pt. grape tomatoes, cut in half
Mustard-Dill Vinaigrette*

1. Cook tortellini according to package directions. Rinse under cold running water.
2. Place sugar snap peas in a small bowl; cover with plastic wrap. Microwave at HIGH 2 minutes. Let stand, covered, 2 minutes. Rinse under cold running water.
3. Thread each skewer with 1 sugar snap pea, 1 tortellini, and 1 tomato half. Place skewers in a 13- x 9-inch baking dish. Pour Mustard-Dill Vinaigrette over skewers, turning to coat. Cover and chill 4 hours. Transfer skewers to a serving platter; discard any remaining vinaigrette. **Yield:** 12 servings.

*1 (12-oz.) bottle light Champagne vinaigrette may be substituted.

To save time, nix the skewers, and toss salad with ½ cup of dressing just before serving. Spoon into a pretty bowl, and garnish with a dill sprig.

mustard-dill vinaigrette

prep: 10 min.

½ cup white wine vinegar
2 Tbsp. chopped fresh dill
3 Tbsp. Dijon mustard
2 pressed garlic cloves
2 tsp. sugar
1¼ cups olive oil
Kosher salt and pepper to taste

1. Whisk together vinegar, dill, mustard, garlic cloves, and sugar. Add 1¼ cups olive oil in a slow, steady stream, whisking constantly until thoroughly combined. Whisk in kosher salt and pepper to taste. **Yield:** 1¾ cups.

Ham-and-Field Pea Salad

prep: 20 min. • **cook: 4 min.** • **other: 9 hr.**

Combining a variety of field peas, such as black-eyed peas, speckled butter beans, and lady peas, gives additional color and texture to this farm-fresh salad.

3 cups fresh or frozen assorted field peas
¼ cup sugar
¼ cup cider vinegar
2 garlic cloves, minced
1 tsp. hot sauce
¾ tsp. salt
¾ tsp. pepper
¼ cup vegetable oil
1 green bell pepper, diced
½ small red onion, diced
1 celery rib, diced
1 cup chopped ham
1 tsp. vegetable oil

1. Prepare peas according to package directions; drain and let cool 1 hour.
2. Whisk together sugar and next 5 ingredients in a large bowl. Add ¼ cup oil in a slow, steady stream, whisking constantly until smooth. Add cooked field peas, bell pepper, onion, and celery, tossing to coat; cover and chill 8 hours.
3. Sauté ham in 1 tsp. hot oil in a small skillet over medium-high heat 4 to 5 minutes or until lightly browned. Stir into pea mixture just before serving.
Yield: 8 servings.

Grilled Shrimp-and-Green Bean Salad

prep: 30 min. • **cook: 8 min.** • **other: 45 min.**

8 (12-inch) wooden skewers
1½ lb. fresh green beans,
   trimmed
2 lb. peeled, medium-size
   raw shrimp
Basil Vinaigrette, divided
6 cooked bacon slices,
   crumbled
1⅓ cups shredded Parmesan
   cheese
¾ cup chopped toasted almonds
Cornbread (optional)

1. Preheat grill to 350° to 400° (medium-high). Soak wooden skewers in water to cover 30 minutes.
2. Cook green beans in boiling salted water to cover 4 minutes or until crisp-tender; drain. Plunge into ice water to stop the cooking process; drain, pat dry, and place in a large bowl.
3. Combine shrimp and ¾ cup Basil Vinaigrette in a large zip-top plastic bag; seal and chill 15 minutes, turning occasionally. Remove shrimp from marinade, discarding marinade. Thread shrimp onto skewers.
4. Grill, covered with grill lid, over 350° to 400° (medium-high) heat 2 minutes on each side or just until shrimp turn pink. Remove shrimp from skewers; toss with green beans, bacon, Parmesan cheese, almonds, and remaining ¾ cup Basil Vinaigrette. Serve over hot cornbread, if desired. **Yield:** 4 to 6 servings.

Toasted cornbread tucked beneath the salad adds a layer of crouton-like crispness.

basil vinaigrette

prep: 10 min.

½ cup balsamic vinegar
½ cup chopped fresh basil
   (about 1 cup packed leaves)
4 large shallots, minced
3 garlic cloves, minced
1 Tbsp. brown sugar
1 tsp. seasoned pepper
½ tsp. salt
1 cup olive oil

1. Whisk together first 7 ingredients in a small bowl until blended; gradually add olive oil, whisking constantly until blended. **Yield:** about 1½ cups.

Rustic Plum Tart

prep: 20 min. • **cook: 46 min.** • **other: 50 min.**

If the plums are very ripe, their juices may ooze out of the tart and onto the parchment paper, but this adds to the dessert's charm.

Parchment paper
Vegetable cooking spray
1½ lb. plums, sliced
½ cup sugar
⅓ cup plum preserves
1 tsp. vanilla extract
¼ tsp. ground allspice
½ (15-oz.) package refrigerated piecrusts
1 Tbsp. all-purpose flour
1 large egg
1 Tbsp. sugar
Sweet Cream Topping (optional)

1. Line baking sheet with parchment paper; coat parchment paper with cooking spray.
2. Preheat oven to 350°. Stir together plums and next 4 ingredients in a large bowl. Let stand 30 minutes, stirring occasionally.
3. Unroll piecrust on prepared baking sheet. Roll into a 12-inch circle.
4. Drain plum mixture, reserving liquid. Toss plums in flour.
5. Mound plums in center of piecrust, leaving a 3-inch border. Fold piecrust border up and over plums, pleating as you go, leaving an opening about 5 inches wide in center.
6. Stir together egg and 1 Tbsp. water. Brush piecrust with egg mixture, and sprinkle with 1 Tbsp. sugar.
7. Bake at 350° for 45 minutes or until filling is bubbly and crust is golden. Carefully transfer tart on parchment paper to a wire rack; cool 20 minutes.
8. Meanwhile, bring reserved plum liquid to a boil in a small saucepan over medium heat. Boil 1 to 2 minutes or until slightly thickened. Let cool slightly. Brush or drizzle 1 to 2 Tbsp. hot plum liquid over exposed fruit in center of tart. Serve immediately with remaining plum syrup, and, if desired, Sweet Cream Topping. **Yield:** 8 servings.

sweet cream topping

prep: 5 min. • **other: 2 hr.**

½ cup sour cream
2 tsp. brown sugar

1. Stir together sour cream and brown sugar. Cover and chill 2 hours before serving. Stir just before serving. **Yield:** ½ cup.

Blackberry Cobbler

prep: 12 min. • **bake: 30 min.**

1 cup sugar
¼ cup all-purpose flour
5 cups fresh blackberries or
 2 (14-oz.) packages frozen
 blackberries, thawed and
 drained
1 Tbsp. lemon juice
Crust
2 Tbsp. butter, melted
1 tsp. sugar
Ice cream (optional)

1. Preheat oven to 425°. Combine 1 cup sugar and flour; add berries, and toss well. (If using frozen berries, increase flour to ⅓ cup.) Sprinkle with lemon juice. Spoon into a greased 8- or 9-inch square baking dish.
2. Prepare Crust, and spoon 9 mounds over blackberries. Brush with butter, and sprinkle with 1 tsp. sugar.
3. Bake, uncovered, at 425° for 30 minutes or until browned and bubbly. Serve warm with ice cream, if desired. **Yield:** 9 servings.

crust

prep: 10 min.

1¾ cups all-purpose flour
3 Tbsp. sugar
1½ tsp. baking powder
¾ tsp. salt
¼ cup shortening
½ cup whipping cream
½ cup buttermilk

1. Combine first 4 ingredients; cut in shortening with a pastry blender until mixture is crumbly. Stir in whipping cream and buttermilk just until blended. **Yield:** enough topping for 1 cobbler.

Grilled Brandied Peach Sundaes

prep: 15 min. • cook: 15 min.

You can also serve this yummy recipe over pound cake.

5   cups sliced peaches
⅓   cup chopped pecans
⅔   cup firmly packed light brown
      sugar
½   tsp. ground cinnamon
¼   tsp. ground nutmeg
1   Tbsp. butter, cut into pieces
3   Tbsp. brandy*
Vanilla ice cream

1. Preheat grill to 300° to 350° (medium). Combine sliced peaches and next 4 ingredients; arrange on center of an 18- x 24-inch sheet of aluminum foil. Top with butter, and drizzle with brandy. Bring edges of foil together over peach mixture, and crimp edges to seal.
2. Place foil package in center of cooking grate. Grill, covered with grill lid, over 300° to 350° (medium) heat 15 minutes or until thoroughly heated.
3. Spoon peach mixture over ice cream, and serve immediately. **Yield:** 10 servings.

*3 Tbsp. apple juice may be substituted.

Grilled Pineapple Slices With Honey-Ginger Glaze

prep: 15 min. • cook: 6 min.

1   medium-size fresh pineapple
2   Tbsp. vegetable oil
½   cup honey
2   Tbsp. fresh lime juice
2   tsp. grated fresh ginger
2   tsp. soy sauce

1. Preheat grill to 300° to 350° (medium). Cut leaves off top of pineapple; cut 1 inch off from each end. Remove and discard core (do not peel). Cut pineapple into ¾-inch-thick slices; brush both sides evenly with oil.
2. Whisk together honey and next 3 ingredients in a small bowl until blended.
3. Grill pineapple slices, covered with grill lid, over 300° to 350° (medium) heat 3 minutes on each side or until grill marks appear. Remove pineapple slices from grill; brush both sides evenly with honey mixture. Serve warm or at room temperature. **Yield:** 4 to 6 servings.

Grilled Brandied
Peach Sundaes

Warm Blackberry Sauce
Over Mango Sorbet

Warm Blackberry Sauce Over Mango Sorbet

prep: 10 min. • **cook: 5 min.**

2   pt. fresh blackberries, halved
¼   cup sugar
2½ tsp. orange zest
½   tsp. ground ginger
1   pt. mango sorbet
6   gingersnaps, crushed

1. Stir together first 4 ingredients in a saucepan over medium heat; cook, stirring constantly, 5 minutes or until thoroughly heated. Serve over sorbet; sprinkle with gingersnaps. **Yield:** 6 servings.

note: For testing purposes only, we used Häagen-Dazs Mango Sorbet.

A small cookie scoop, available at discount stores, will let you portion the sorbet evenly, giving your guests just a little something sweet after the meal.

Blueberry Bread Pudding

prep: 15 min. • **cook: 1 hr.** • **other: 8 hr., 5 min.**

1   (16-oz.) French bread loaf, cubed
1   (8-oz.) package cream cheese, cut into pieces
3   cups fresh blueberries, divided
6   large eggs
4   cups milk
½   cup sugar
¼   cup butter, melted
¼   cup maple syrup
1   (10-oz.) jar blueberry preserves
Garnishes: fresh mint leaves, edible pansies

1. Preheat oven to 350°. Arrange half of bread cubes in a lightly greased 13- x 9-inch pan. Sprinkle evenly with cream cheese and 1 cup blueberries; top with remaining bread cubes.
2. Whisk together eggs, 4 cups milk, sugar, butter, and maple syrup; pour over bread mixture, pressing bread cubes to absorb egg mixture. Cover and chill 8 hours.
3. Bake, covered, at 350° for 30 minutes. Uncover and bake 30 more minutes or until lightly browned and set. Let stand 5 minutes before serving.
4. Stir together remaining 2 cups blueberries and blueberry preserves in a saucepan over low heat until warm. Serve blueberry mixture over bread pudding. Garnish, if desired. **Yield:** 8 servings.

A chunky blueberry sauce crowns each serving of this blueberry laced bread pudding.

Peach-Pecan Ice Cream

prep: 40 min. • **cook: 25 min.** • **other: 1 hr.**

For best results, make this recipe midsummer when peaches are at their prime. Homemade ice cream can be frozen up to 2 months in a freezer container that has a tight-fitting lid.

6   cups mashed ripe peaches (about 2½ lb.)
1   cup sugar
3   large eggs
1½ cups sugar
2   Tbsp. all-purpose flour
½   tsp. salt
4   cups milk
1   cup whipping cream
1   Tbsp. vanilla extract
1   cup chopped pecans

1. Combine peaches and 1 cup sugar; stir well, and set aside.

2. Beat eggs at medium speed with an electric mixer until frothy. Combine 1½ cups sugar, flour, and salt; stir well. Gradually add sugar mixture to eggs; beat until thickened. Gradually add milk; beat until blended.

3. Pour custard mixture into a large heavy saucepan. Cook over medium-low heat, stirring constantly, until thickend and coats the back of a metal spoon (about 25 minutes). Remove from heat, and set pan over a bowl of ice water; stir gently until cool. Stir in peaches, whipping cream, vanilla, and pecans.

4. Pour mixture into freezer container of a 1-gal. hand-turned or electric freezer. Freeze according to manufacturer's instructions. Pack freezer with additional ice and rock salt, and let sit 1 hour before serving. **Yield:** 11 cups.

Tomato-Watermelon Sorbet

Tomato-Watermelon Sorbet

prep: 20 min.   •   **other:** 30 min.

6   cups (1-inch) seeded ripe watermelon chunks
1   cup sugar
¼   tsp. salt
6   very ripe large tomatoes, quartered (about 3½ lb.)
2   Tbsp. fresh lemon juice
Coarse salt (optional)

1. Combine first 3 ingredients in a large bowl; stir well. Let stand 30 minutes.

2. Squeeze tomato quarters into a wire-mesh strainer over a 4-cup measuring cup. Place squeezed tomatoes into strainer, and firmly press with back of a spoon, pressing until liquid measures 3 cups. Discard tomato pulp in strainer.

3. Process half of tomato juice and half of watermelon mixture in a blender until smooth. Repeat with remaining tomato juice and watermelon. Stir in lemon juice. Pour mixture into freezer container of a 2½-qt. electric ice-cream maker, and freeze according to manufacturer's instructions. (Instructions and times will vary.) Sprinkle each serving with coarse salt, if desired. **Yield:** about 2 qt.

Chef Bill Smith at Crook's Corner Café & Bar in Chapel Hill, North Carolina, developed this fresh treat using only five ingredients.

Raspberry-Buttermilk Sherbet

prep: 20 min.   •   **other:** about 30 min.

2   cups fresh raspberries*
1   cup sugar
2   cups buttermilk
1   tsp. vanilla extract
Garnishes: fresh mint sprigs, fresh raspberries

1. Process raspberries in a food processor or blender until smooth, stopping to scrape down sides. Press raspberry purée through a fine wire-mesh strainer into a large bowl, discarding solids. Add sugar, buttermilk, and 1 tsp. vanilla extract to bowl, and stir until well blended.

2. Pour raspberry mixture into freezer container of a 4-qt. ice-cream maker, and freeze according to manufacturer's instructions. Garnish each serving, if desired. **Yield:** about 4 cups.

*1 (14-oz.) package frozen raspberries, thawed, may be substituted.

You can use this same recipe to make Blueberry-Buttermilk Sherbet; just substitute an equal amount of fresh or frozen blueberries for raspberries.

Biscotti With Lavender and Orange

prep: 13 min. • **cook: 50 min.**

Store biscotti in an airtight container. It also freezes well up to 6 months.

¼ cup sugar
¼ cup butter, softened
1½ to 2 Tbsp. coarsely chopped fresh lavender
½ tsp. orange zest
2 large eggs
2 cups all-purpose flour
2 tsp. baking powder
½ tsp. salt
½ cup sliced almonds, toasted
½ tsp. vanilla extract

1. Preheat oven to 350°. Beat first 4 ingredients at medium speed with an electric mixer until well blended. Add eggs, 1 at a time, beating until blended.

2. Combine flour, baking powder, and salt. Gradually add flour mixture to sugar mixture, beating until blended. Stir in almonds and vanilla.

3. Turn dough out onto a lightly greased baking sheet. Shape dough into a 10-inch log; flatten to 1-inch thickness. Bake at 350° for 30 minutes. Remove from baking sheet, and cool completely on a wire rack. Reduce oven temperature to 300°.

4. Cut log diagonally into ½-inch-thick slices using a serrated knife. Place slices on an ungreased baking sheet. Bake at 300° for 20 to 25 minutes (cookies will be slightly soft in center but will harden as they cool).

5. Remove from baking sheet; cool completely on wire rack. **Yield:** 15 servings.

biscotti step-by-step

1. Shape dough into a log for the first baking. 2. Cool cookie log on a wire rack.
3. Cut log diagonally into ½-inch slices, and then bake the logs until crisp.

autumn harvest

Warm Cranberry Brie

prep: 10 min. • **cook: 10 min.**

¼ cup chopped pecans
1 (16-oz.) Brie round
1 (16-oz.) can whole-berry cranberry sauce
¼ cup firmly packed brown sugar
2 Tbsp. spiced rum*
½ tsp. ground nutmeg
Assorted crackers, apple slices, pear slices

1. Preheat oven to 350°. Bake pecans in a single layer in a shallow pan 5 minutes or until toasted and fragrant.
2. Trim rind from top of Brie, leaving a ⅓-inch border on top. Place Brie on a baking sheet. Stir together cranberry sauce and next 3 ingredients; spread mixture evenly over top of Brie round.
3. Bake Brie at 350° for 5 minutes. Remove from oven, and sprinkle with chopped toasted pecans. Serve with assorted crackers and apple and pear slices. **Yield:** 8 appetizer servings.

*2 Tbsp. orange juice may be substituted.

Dip into this luscious melted cheese with your choice of crackers or fresh slices of pear or apple. Toasted pecans add a pleasant crunch.

tips from our kitchen

Cooking with Brie Brie has a fairly short life, so use it within a few days. Avoid buying Brie that smells of ammonia because it may be overripe. To keep Brie fresher longer, wrap it in parchment or wax paper, and refrigerate. Plastic wrap hastens its demise.

Sugar-and-Spice Nuts

prep: 15 min. • **cook: 50 min.** • **other: 30 min.**

¾ cup sugar
1 Tbsp. Sweet Spice Blend
¾ tsp. salt
1 egg white
1 lb. pecan halves*

1. Preheat oven to 275°. Stir together first 3 ingredients in a medium bowl.
2. Beat egg white and 1 Tbsp. water in a medium bowl using a handheld mixer or a wire whisk until foamy. (No liquid should remain.) Add pecans, stirring until evenly coated.
3. Add pecans to sugar mixture, stirring until evenly coated. Place pecans in a single layer on a buttered 15- x 10-inch jelly-roll pan.
4. Bake at 275° for 50 to 55 minutes, stirring every 15 minutes. Immediately spread in a single layer on wax paper; cool 30 minutes or until completely cool. Store in an airtight container. **Yield:** about 5 cups.

*Whole almonds or walnut halves may be substituted.

sweet spice blend

prep: 5 min.

2 Tbsp. light brown sugar
2 Tbsp. ground cinnamon
4 tsp. dried ground ginger
1 tsp. ground nutmeg
½ tsp. ground cloves
½ tsp. ground cardamom

1. Stir together all ingredients in a small bowl. Store in an airtight container. **Yield:** 6 Tbsp.

tips from the farm

Storing Pecans Unshelled pecans are at their peak in autumn months. Pecans in the shell will stay fresh in a cool, dry place up to 6 months. Shelled pecans can be kept in an airtight container in the refrigerator up to 1 year or in the freezer for 2 years or longer.

Fig, Prosciutto, and Blue Cheese Squares

prep: 14 min.   •   cook: 26 min.   •   other: 5 min.

2   Tbsp. olive oil

2   garlic cloves, pressed

3   oz. thinly sliced prosciutto, chopped

1   (11-oz.) can refrigerated thin pizza crust dough

1   Tbsp. chopped fresh rosemary

½   cup fig preserves

¾   cup crumbled blue cheese

½   tsp. freshly ground pepper

1. Preheat oven to 400°. Combine oil and garlic in a small microwave-safe bowl. Microwave at HIGH 20 seconds or just until warm. Let stand while prosciutto cooks.

2. Cook prosciutto in a large skillet over medium-high heat 11 minutes or until browned and crisp; remove prosciutto, and drain on paper towels.

3. Unroll dough, and place on a lightly greased large baking sheet. Press out dough with hands to form a 15- x 13-inch rectangle. Brush dough with garlic-flavored oil; sprinkle rosemary over dough. Spread fig preserves over dough. Sprinkle with prosciutto, cheese, and pepper.

4. Bake at 400° for 15 minutes or until crust is browned and crisp. Let stand 5 minutes before cutting. **Yield:** 3 dozen.

Refrigerated pizza crust dough unrolls to almost the perfect dimensions needed for this recipe. Briefly heating the oil and garlic infuses the oil with garlic flavor before it is brushed on the dough. This is a uniquely flavored appetizer pizza not to be missed.

Pancetta Crisps With Goat Cheese and Pear

prep: 15 min. • **cook: 8 min.** • **other: 10 min.**

Often called "Italian bacon," pancetta adds a flavorful, slightly salty layer to this savory appetizer.

12 thin slices pancetta (about ⅓ lb.)
1 Bartlett pear
½ (4-oz.) package goat cheese, crumbled
Freshly cracked pepper
Honey
Garnish: fresh thyme sprigs

1. Preheat oven to 450°. Arrange pancetta slices in a single layer on an aluminum foil-lined baking sheet.
2. Bake at 450° for 8 to 10 minutes or until golden. Transfer to a paper towel-lined wire rack using a spatula. Let stand 10 minutes or until crisp.
3. Core pear with an apple corer. Cut pear crosswise into 12 thin rings. Arrange on a serving platter. Top evenly with pancetta and goat cheese; sprinkle with pepper. Drizzle with honey just before serving. Garnish, if desired. **Yield:** 6 servings.

Rosemary-Lemon Olives

prep: 4 min. • **cook: 40 min.**

Use the infused oil resulting from this recipe as a dipping oil for crusty baguette slices.

6 (5-inch) strips lemon peel
2 (8-inch) fresh rosemary sprigs
⅛ tsp. dried crushed red pepper
1 cup kalamata olives
1 cup Sicilian olives
1 cup extra virgin olive oil
Garnish: fresh rosemary

1. Preheat oven to 300°. Place lemon peel, rosemary, and red pepper flakes in an 11- x 7-inch baking dish. Add olives, and drizzle with olive oil. Bake, uncovered, at 300° for 40 minutes. Cool to room temperature. Garnish, if desired, and serve immediately, or store in refrigerator up to 5 days. Bring refrigerated olives to room temperature before serving. **Yield:** 2 cups.

Pancetta Crisps With
Goat Cheese and Pear

Maple Coffee

prep: 5 min. • **cook: 5 min.**

2 cups half-and-half
½ cup maple syrup
2 cups hot brewed coffee
Sweetened whipped cream

1. Cook half-and-half and maple syrup in a saucepan over medium heat, stirring constantly, until thoroughly heated. (Do not boil.) Stir in coffee, and serve with sweetened whipped cream. **Yield:** 4½ cups.

note: This recipe easily doubles for a larger crowd. To make sweetened whipped cream, use 1 to 2 Tbsp. sugar to 1 cup whipping cream.

The darker the color of maple syrup, the stronger the flavor. The lightest syrup has the most delicate flavor and is the most expensive. When buying maple syrup, always look for the word "pure" on the label.

Açaí Berry Mulled Cider

prep: 7 min. • **cook: 1 hr.**

The açaí raspberry juice blend in this brew features açaí juice, a now readily available superfood packed with powerful antioxidants. Mix it with farm-fresh apple cider and autumn spices for a soothing seasonal beverage.

2   (1.5-liter) bottles apple cider
6   cups açaí-raspberry juice blend
⅓   cup firmly packed light brown sugar
3   (3-inch) cinnamon sticks
5   whole allspice
5   whole cloves
1   (1-inch) piece fresh ginger, peeled
3 orange slices
3 lemon slices

1. Combine first 3 ingredients in a very large Dutch oven. Cook over medium-high heat, stirring until sugar dissolves.

2. Tie cinnamon sticks and next 3 ingredients in a cheesecloth bag; add spice bag to cider. Add orange and lemon slices. Bring mixture to a boil; reduce heat to medium-low, and simmer 45 minutes. Discard spice bag. **Yield:** 18½ cups.

note: For testing purposes only, we used Tropicana Pure Raspberry Açaí.

Ginger Tea

prep: 15 min. • **cook: 5 min.** • **other: 5 min.**

To make this tea, look for knobs of fresh ginger at a farmers market or in the produce section of a grocery store. Peel the brown skin, and grate the fibrous pulp for this surprisingly spicy tea. Enjoy this tea served over ice, or it's great hot too.

⅓   to ½ cup grated fresh ginger
⅓   cup lemon juice
¼   cup honey
4   regular-size green tea bags
1½ cups sugar

1. Combine first 3 ingredients with 2 qt. water in a Dutch oven; bring to a boil. Reduce heat, and simmer 5 minutes, stirring occasionally. Remove from heat.

2. Add tea bags; cover and steep 5 minutes. Remove tea bags; stir in sugar, and cool.

3. Pour tea through a wire-mesh strainer into a pitcher; serve over ice. **Yield:** 8 cups.

Beef Brisket With Fall Vegetables

prep: 18 min. • **cook: 12 hr.**

2 (2-lb.) beef briskets, trimmed

2 tsp. salt

1 tsp. pepper

1 Tbsp. vegetable oil

4 carrots, peeled and cut into
   2-inch pieces

3 parsnips, peeled and sliced

2 celery ribs, sliced

1 large onion, sliced

1 fennel bulb, quartered

12 fresh thyme sprigs

1 (1-oz.) envelope dry onion
   soup mix

1 (14-oz.) can low-sodium beef
   broth

¾ cup dry red wine

½ cup ketchup

2 Tbsp. Beau Monde seasoning

8 garlic cloves

¾ cup chopped fresh parsley

Garnish: fresh thyme sprigs

1. Sprinkle beef with salt and pepper.

2. Heat oil over medium-high heat in a large non-stick skillet. Add beef; cook 4 minutes on each side or until browned. Transfer beef to a 6-qt. slow cooker. Add carrot and next 5 ingredients.

3. Whisk together soup mix and next 6 ingredients. Pour mixture evenly over beef.

4. Cover and cook on LOW 12 hours or until tender. Transfer beef to a serving platter. Pour remaining vegetable mixture through a wire-mesh strainer, reserving juices, carrot, and onion; discard remaining vegetable mixture. Serve beef and vegetables with juices. Garnish, if desired. **Yield:** 8 servings.

This slow-cooker specialty pairs beef brisket with some of autumns finest produce for a delectable comfort-food dish.

Black-eyed Pea Cakes With Cranberry–Red Pepper Salsa

prep: 27 min. • cook: 3 min. per batch

2 (15.83-oz.) cans black-eyed peas, rinsed, drained, and divided
1 large egg
1 tsp. ground cumin
¾ tsp. salt
1¼ cups panko (Japanese breadcrumbs), divided
½ cup bottled roasted red peppers, drained and chopped
⅓ cup chopped red onion
⅓ cup chopped fresh cilantro
3 Tbsp. all-purpose flour
2 garlic cloves, minced
Peanut oil for frying
Cranberry–Red Pepper Salsa

1. Process 1½ cups black-eyed peas in a food processor until coarsely chopped.
2. Whisk together egg, cumin, and salt in a large bowl. Add chopped peas, remaining whole peas, ¾ cup breadcrumbs, and next 5 ingredients; stir well to combine. Place remaining ½ cup breadcrumbs in a shallow dish. Using a ¼ cup measure, shape pea mixture into a cake; dredge in breadcrumbs. Repeat with remaining mixture and breadcrumbs. Place cakes on a baking sheet lined with plastic wrap; cover and chill overnight.
3. Pour oil to a depth of 1 inch into a large skillet, and heat to 350°.
4. Fry cakes, in batches, 3 minutes or until golden. Drain well on paper towels. Serve immediately with Cranberry–Red Pepper Salsa. **Yield:** 12 appetizer or 6 entrée servings.

If you won't be serving all the Black-eyed Pea Cakes at once, freeze uncooked cakes; then thaw before dredging in breadcrumbs and frying. The salsa can be made up to 3 days before serving.

cranberry–red pepper salsa

prep: 15 min.

1½ cups fresh or frozen cranberries, thawed
½ cup bottled roasted red bell peppers, drained and chopped
3 Tbsp. honey
½ tsp. lime zest
2 Tbsp. lime juice
1 green onion, chopped
1 jalapeño pepper, seeded and minced
2 Tbsp. chopped fresh cilantro

1. Process cranberries in a food processor until coarsely chopped; transfer to a bowl. Add bell peppers and remaining ingredients, stirring well to combine. Cover and chill until ready to serve. Serve cold or at room temperature. **Yield:** 2 cups.

Eggplant Parmesan

prep: 35 min. · **cook: 1 hr., 9 min.**

Sometimes eggplant tastes a little bitter; this can be remedied by salting and letting it sit for about 20 minutes. Eggplant also has a tendency to soak up oil, so coat with a batter or crumb mixture before it's fried.

3   large eggs
1½ cups Italian-seasoned breadcrumbs or panko (Japanese breadcrumbs)
¼   cup grated Parmesan cheese
2   large eggplants, cut into 18 (½-inch-thick) slices
3   Tbsp. olive oil, divided
½   cup grated Parmesan cheese, divided
1   (8-oz.) package shredded mozzarella cheese, divided
3   cups Pasta Sauce

1. Whisk together eggs and 3 Tbsp. water until blended.

2. Combine breadcrumbs and ¼ cup Parmesan cheese.

3. Dip eggplant slices into egg mixture; dredge in breadcrumb mixture. Preheat oven to 375°.

4. Cook eggplant, in 3 batches, in 1 Tbsp. hot oil (per batch) in a large skillet over medium heat 4 minutes on each side or until tender.

5. Arrange one-third of eggplant in a single layer in a lightly greased 11- x 7-inch baking dish. Sprinkle with 2 Tbsp. Parmesan cheese and ½ cup mozzarella cheese. Repeat layers twice. Spoon 3 cups Pasta Sauce over top.

6. Bake, covered, at 375° for 35 minutes. Uncover and sprinkle with remaining ½ cup mozzarella cheese and remaining 2 Tbsp. Parmesan cheese. Bake 10 more minutes or until cheese melts. **Yield:** 8 servings.

pasta sauce

prep: 15 min. · **cook: 2 hr., 10 min.**

2   small onions, chopped
4   garlic cloves, chopped
¼   cup vegetable oil
2   (28-oz.) cans diced tomatoes, undrained
2   (12-oz.) cans tomato paste
¼   cup sugar
2   Tbsp. dried Italian seasoning
1   Tbsp. salt
1   Tbsp. dried basil
2   tsp. black pepper
1   tsp. dried crushed red pepper

1. Sauté onion and garlic in hot oil in a Dutch oven over medium heat 10 minutes or until onion is tender. Stir in 8 cups water and remaining ingredients. Bring to a boil; reduce heat, and simmer, stirring often, 2 hours. Divide into 1 cup portions; set aside 3 cups for Eggplant Parmesan, and freeze remaining portions. **Yield:** 12 cups.

Ragoût of Mushrooms With Creamy Polenta

prep: 15 min. • cook: 13 min.

1 cup halved and thinly sliced shallots
3 garlic cloves, minced
4 Tbsp. olive oil
2 (8-oz.) packages sliced baby portobello mushrooms*
2 (3.5-oz.) packages fresh shiitake mushrooms, stemmed and sliced
½ cup port wine
1 cup chicken broth
¼ cup fresh flat-leaf parsley, chopped
4 Tbsp. butter
1½ Tbsp. fresh thyme leaves
¾ tsp. salt
½ tsp. pepper
Creamy Polenta
Freshly shaved Parmesan cheese
Garnish: fresh thyme sprigs

1. Sauté shallots and garlic in hot oil in a large skillet over medium heat 2 minutes. Increase heat to medium-high, add mushrooms, and cook, stirring constantly, 4 to 5 minutes. Stir in wine; cook 2 minutes. Stir in broth and next 5 ingredients. Reduce heat to low, and simmer 5 minutes or until slightly thickened.

2. Serve over Creamy Polenta with shaved Parmesan cheese. Garnish, if desired. **Yield:** 6 servings.

*2 (8-oz.) packages sliced fresh button mushrooms may be substituted.

If you don't have port, it's okay to substitute your favorite red wine in this dish. Look for polenta in the gourmet or international section of the grocery store. When cooking polenta, don't let it boil, or it will spatter.

creamy polenta

prep: 5 min. • cook: 7 min.

7 cups chicken broth, divided
2 cups polenta
1 (8-oz.) package ⅓-less-fat cream cheese

1. Bring 6 cups chicken broth to a light boil in a Dutch oven over medium-high heat; slowly stir in polenta. Reduce heat to low, and cook, stirring constantly, 2 to 3 minutes or until polenta thickens. (Do not boil.) Stir in cream cheese until blended. Stir in remaining chicken broth. Cover and keep warm. **Yield:** 6 servings.

Yukon Gold Mash With Morel Sauce

prep: 15 min. • **cook:** 25 min.

This alluring entrée has three parts: a roasted mushroom cap as its base, a buttery mashed potato middle, and an unctuous mushroom sauce that's like meat—which, by the way, you won't miss.

Morel Sauce
6   medium Yukon gold potatoes, peeled and coarsely chopped (about 2½ lb.)
Roasted Portobello Caps
2   garlic cloves, sliced
¼   cup butter, melted
1¼ cups milk
1   tsp. salt
½   tsp. freshly ground pepper
Garnish: fresh thyme sprigs

1. Prepare Morel Sauce.
2. Cook chopped potatoes in boiling salted water to cover 20 minutes or until tender. Drain potatoes, and set aside.
3. Meanwhile, prepare Roasted Portobello Caps.
4. Sauté garlic in butter in a large saucepan over medium heat until butter and garlic are golden. Add milk, salt, and pepper. Bring to a simmer; remove from heat, and add potatoes. Mash with a potato masher until almost smooth.
5. To serve, spoon Yukon Gold Mash into Roasted Portobello Caps; top with Morel Sauce. Garnish, if desired. **Yield:** 6 servings.

morel sauce

prep: 15 min. • **cook: 17 min.** • **other: 5 min.**

3 (½-oz.) packages dried
   morel mushrooms, rinsed
   and drained
2 cups boiling water
2 Tbsp. butter
2 Tbsp. olive oil
2 cups (8 oz.) coarsely chopped
   fresh mushrooms
¾ cup finely chopped onion
¾ cup port wine
2 Tbsp. balsamic vinegar
¼ cup all-purpose flour
½ cup half-and-half
1½ Tbsp. chopped fresh sage
1 tsp. salt
½ tsp. freshly ground pepper

1. Place morels in 2 cups boiling water; let stand 5 minutes. Remove morels with a slotted spoon, reserving broth. Strain broth, discarding any sandy residue in bottom of pan. Chop morels. Set morels and broth aside.

2. Heat butter and oil in a large, deep skillet over medium-high heat until butter melts. Add fresh mushrooms and onion. Cook, stirring constantly, 5 minutes or until onion is browned; add morels, wine, and vinegar. Reduce heat, and simmer, uncovered, 2 minutes. Add reserved broth; bring to a boil, reduce heat, and simmer, uncovered, 3 minutes.

3. Combine flour and ½ cup water, stirring until smooth. Add to mushroom mixture. Cook, stirring constantly, 2 minutes or until thickened and smooth. Stir in half-and-half and remaining ingredients. Cook 5 minutes. Serve over Yukon Gold Mash. **Yield:** 4 cups.

roasted portobello caps

prep: 3 min. • **cook: 15 min.**

6 portobello mushroom caps
3 to 4 Tbsp. olive oil
1 tsp. salt
1 tsp. freshly ground pepper

1. Preheat oven to 450°. Place mushroom caps in a large bowl. Drizzle with oil and sprinkle with salt and pepper. Toss gently, being careful not to tear mushrooms. Arrange mushrooms, cavity side down, in a single layer in a jelly-roll pan or shallow roasting pan.

2. Roast at 450° for 15 minutes, turning once. **Yield:** 6 servings.

Fresh Vegetable Penne

prep: 25 min. • cook: 51 min.

1 (2-lb.) butternut squash, peeled and cut into 1½-inch cubes

Vegetable cooking spray

1 Tbsp. olive oil, divided

¾ tsp. salt, divided

½ tsp. freshly ground black pepper, divided

1 cup chopped leek (about 1 medium)

½ tsp. minced fresh garlic

1½ cups vegetable or chicken broth

½ cup fat-free half-and-half

16 oz. uncooked penne pasta

½ cup frozen baby sweet peas

1 Tbsp. chopped fresh sage leaves

⅛ to ¼ tsp. dried crushed red pepper

¼ cup shredded Italian three-cheese blend

Garnish: fresh sage leaves

1. Preheat oven to 425°. Place squash cubes on a large aluminum foil-lined jelly-roll pan coated with cooking spray. Drizzle squash with 1 tsp. oil, and sprinkle with ¼ tsp. salt and ¼ tsp. black pepper. Toss to coat.

2. Bake at 425° for 25 to 30 minutes or until squash is tender and golden, stirring occasionally.

3. Heat remaining 2 tsp. oil in a large nonstick skillet over medium-high heat; add leek, and sauté 5 minutes or until tender and lightly browned. Add garlic; sauté 1 minute. Remove from heat, and set aside.

4. Process cooked butternut squash, vegetable broth, and half-and-half in a food processor until smooth.

5. Cook pasta according to package directions, omitting salt and oil. Add peas to boiling water during last 2 minutes of cooking time; drain. Return pasta and peas to pan. Stir in leek mixture, remaining ½ tsp. salt, remaining ¼ tsp. black pepper, 1 Tbsp. chopped sage, and crushed red pepper. Add processed squash mixture, tossing to coat. Sprinkle with Italian three-cheese blend. Garnish, if desired, and serve immediately. **Yield:** 6 servings.

tips from the farm

Winter Squash 101 Winter squash are generally available year-round, but are best in fall and winter months; they are allowed to mature until their flesh is thick and their shells are hard, and therefore require longer cooking. Whole winter squash can be kept for months in a cool, dark place; if cut, they can be refrigerated up to a week. Butternut squash is packed with vitamins A and D, and is especially good for baking and pureeing.

Sweet Potato–Peanut Soup With Ham Croutons

prep: 23 min.   cook: 45 min.

The peanut flavor in this thick, rich appetizer soup comes from creamy peanut butter. The crisp ham croutons are addictive.

¼ cup butter
1 medium onion, chopped
¾ cup chopped celery
2 garlic cloves, chopped
6 cups chicken broth
3 lb. sweet potatoes, peeled and coarsely chopped
1 Tbsp. chopped fresh rosemary
2 cups cubed cooked ham
⅔ cup creamy peanut butter
1 cup whipping cream
1 tsp. salt
¼ tsp. freshly ground pepper
Garnish: fresh rosemary sprigs

1. Melt butter in a Dutch oven over medium heat. Add onion, celery, and garlic; sauté 10 minutes or until tender. Add broth, potato, and chopped rosemary. Bring to a boil; cover, reduce heat, and simmer 25 minutes or until potato is very tender.
2. Meanwhile, heat a large nonstick skillet over medium-high heat. Add ham, and cook until browned and crisp on all sides. Remove from heat; set aside.
3. Process potato mixture, in batches, in a food processor or blender until smooth. Return to Dutch oven; stir in peanut butter. Cook over medium-low heat until smooth, stirring often. Stir in cream, salt, and pepper; cook until thoroughly heated.
4. To serve, ladle into individual bowls. Top each serving with ham. Garnish, if desired. **Yield:** 10 servings.

Caramelized Onion-and-Mushroom Bisque

prep: 15 min. • **cook: 54 min.** • **other: 30 min.**

2   Tbsp. butter

3   lb. onions, sliced and
     separated into rings

2   garlic cloves, chopped

4½ cups vegetable broth, divided

2   Tbsp. olive oil

4   (3.5-oz.) packages shiitake
     mushrooms, stems removed
     and sliced

½   tsp. salt

½   cup whipping cream

2   Tbsp. dry sherry

1   Tbsp. fresh lemon juice

¼   tsp. salt

⅛   tsp. ground white pepper

Sour cream (optional)

1. Melt butter in a Dutch oven over medium heat; add onions. Cook over medium heat, stirring occasionally, 35 minutes or until onion is lightly browned and very tender. Add garlic, and cook 1 minute. Add 1 cup broth, stirring to loosen browned bits from bottom of pan (can make ahead to this point. Remove onions from heat; cover and chill until ready to prepare remainder of soup). Stir in 2 cups broth; bring to a boil. Cover, reduce heat, and simmer 10 minutes. Remove from heat, and let cool 30 minutes.

2. Meanwhile, heat oil in a large skillet over medium-high heat. Add mushrooms, and cook 8 to 10 minutes, stirring once or twice, until mushrooms are lightly browned and liquid has evaporated; stir in ½ tsp. salt. Remove from heat, and set aside.

3. Process soup, in batches, in a blender or food processor 2 minutes or until smooth, stopping to scrape down sides. Return to Dutch oven. Stir in remaining 1½ cups broth and whipping cream; bring to a boil. Remove from heat; stir in sherry, lemon juice, ¼ tsp. salt, and pepper.

4. To serve, ladle soup into individual bowls, and top evenly with mushrooms; dollop each with sour cream, if desired. **Yield:** 7 servings.

To jump-start this recipe, begin a day ahead and caramelize the onions up to the point of adding 2 cups of broth.

Homemade Applesauce

prep: 20 min. • cook: 20 min.

For the best taste and texture, use a variety of apples—such as Granny Smith, Golden Delicious, and Gala—when making applesauce and apple pie. Stir in a little chopped rosemary, and serve this applesauce as a side dish with pork chops or hash browns.

12 large apples, peeled and coarsely chopped
1 cup sugar
½ lemon, sliced

1. Cook all ingredients in a Dutch oven over medium heat, stirring often, 20 minutes or until apples are tender and juices are thickened. Remove and discard lemon slices. Serve applesauce warm; or let cool and store in an airtight container in the refrigerator for up to 1 week. **Yield:** about 6 cups.

Spiced Applesauce: Substitute ½ cup firmly packed brown sugar and ½ cup granulated sugar for 1 cup sugar. Omit lemon slices, and add 1 tsp. ground cinnamon and ¼ tsp. ground cloves; prepare as directed.

Apple-Raisin Dressing

prep: 16 min. • cook: 1 hr., 3 min.

If you're a fan of moist dressing, use the larger amount of broth.

¼ cup butter
1 large onion, diced
2 celery ribs, diced (about 1 cup)
2 Granny Smith apples, diced (about 3 cups)
2 tsp. rubbed sage
½ tsp. salt
¼ tsp. freshly ground black pepper
1 (16-oz.) package herb-seasoned stuffing mix
1 cup golden raisins
1 cup chopped pecans, toasted
2½ to 3 cups chicken broth
2 large eggs, lightly beaten

1. Preheat oven to 325°. Melt butter in a large skillet over medium-high heat. Add onion and celery, and sauté 10 minutes or until tender. Add apple; sauté 3 minutes or until tender. Stir in sage, salt, and pepper.
2. Combine sautéed mixture, stuffing, raisins, and pecans in a large bowl. Add chicken broth and eggs; stir well. Spoon dressing into a lightly greased 13- x 9-inch baking dish. Bake, uncovered, at 325° for 50 to 60 minutes or until well browned. **Yield:** 10 to 12 servings.

Homemade Applesauce

Broccoli With Caramelized Garlic and Pine Nuts

prep: 5 min. • **cook: 15 min.**

⅓ cup pine nuts
¼ cup butter
1 Tbsp. olive oil
6 garlic cloves, thinly sliced
1 lb. broccoli florets
½ tsp. salt
⅛ tsp. dried crushed red pepper

1. Toast pine nuts in a large skillet over medium heat 6 minutes or until lightly browned. Remove from skillet, and set aside.

2. Heat butter and oil in same skillet over medium heat until butter melts. Add garlic, and sauté 1 to 2 minutes or until lightly browned. Add broccoli, salt, and crushed red pepper. Sauté 8 minutes or until broccoli is tender. Stir in pine nuts before serving. **Yield:** 6 servings.

For convenience, you can use bagged broccoli florets for this recipe.

tips from the farm

Broccoli by the Head Fresh broccoli is at its peak from October through April. Look for firm stalks with tightly bunched heads. If the heads show signs of buds beginning to turn yellow, it's over the hill. Refrigerate fresh broccoli in a plastic bag up to 4 days. To revive limp broccoli, trim ½ inch from the base of the stalk and set the stalk in a glass of cold water in the refrigerator overnight.

Edwin Marty, Organic Farmer

Jones Valley Urban Farm, Birmingham, Alabama

Jones Valley Urban Farm (JVUF) Executive Director, Edwin Marty, knows his local produce. He and others at JVUF—a community-based nonprofit organic farm—are part of a growing movement that promotes buying and eating area-grown produce.

Eating local, as it's called, tastes and feels right for so many reasons. "The food that you are going to buy from local farmers is going to have so many more nutrients because it is picked ripe," says Edwin. "It is picked when it's ready to be eaten, when the sun's energy has given it the maximum amount of flavor and sweetness."

As if freshness, great flavor, and seasonal variety aren't enough to make you want to pull up a chair at the "eat local" table, then consider its economic impact. When you buy from area farmers, more of your food dollars stay in your community.

"People really can't imagine the implications of that," says Edwin. "When you buy something that wasn't produced in your area from a megamart, something like 10 cents stays in your community. If you go to the farmers market and pay a local farmer $1 for corn, 95% of that dollar stays in your area."

So the next time you need to make a grocery run, do your community and yourself a favor, and consider eating local. For more information about JVUF, visit www.jvuf.org.

Brussels Sprouts With Marmalade Glaze

prep: 10 min. • cook: 36 min.

2 lb. fresh Brussels sprouts
1 (32-oz.) container chicken
   broth
2 Tbsp. butter
½ cup minced onion
2 garlic cloves, minced
½ cup orange marmalade
¼ tsp. salt
¼ tsp. pepper

1. Wash Brussels sprouts thoroughly, and remove any discolored leaves. Trim stem ends. Place Brussels sprouts in a large saucepan; add broth. Bring to a boil over medium-high heat; reduce heat, and simmer 5 minutes or until desired tenderness.

2. Drain Brussels sprouts, reserving 1 cup chicken broth. Melt butter in saucepan; add onion and garlic. Sauté over medium-high heat 2 minutes or until tender. Add reserved broth and marmalade; bring to a simmer. Cook, stirring often, 15 minutes or until glaze reduces and thickens. Add Brussels sprouts, salt, and pepper; toss well until thoroughly heated. Serve warm. **Yield:** 6 servings.

For the best-tasting Brussels sprouts, choose small sprouts that are firm and bright green.

Roasted Cauliflower
With Pine Nuts and Raisins

prep: 20 min. • cook: 22 min. • other: 5 min.

The natural sugars in some produce, such as cauliflower, potatoes, squash, and peppers, cause them to brown, or caramelize, when roasted.

¼ cup golden raisins
1 head cauliflower (about 2 lb.)
¼ cup pine nuts
2 Tbsp. olive oil
1 tsp. chopped fresh or ½ tsp. dried thyme
½ tsp. salt
¼ tsp. pepper
1 Tbsp. butter
1 large garlic clove, pressed
¼ cup panko (Japanese breadcrumbs)

1. Preheat oven to 400°. Cover raisins with hot water in a small bowl; let stand 5 minutes or until plump. Drain.

2. Cut cauliflower into equal-size florets. Toss together florets, pine nuts, olive oil, and thyme in a jelly-roll pan. Spread in single layer, and season with salt and pepper.

3. Bake at 400° for 20 minutes or until edges of cauliflower are caramelized and nuts are toasted. Remove from oven. Increase oven temperature to broil.

4. Microwave butter with garlic in a small glass bowl at HIGH 30 seconds. Stir in raisins and breadcrumbs. Toss raisin mixture with cauliflower mixture in jelly-roll pan, and spread mixture in a single layer.

5. Broil 6 inches from heat 2 minutes or just until golden. Serve immediately. **Yield:** 4 servings.

tips from the farm

Storing Cauliflower To store fresh cauliflower, wrap it in plastic wrap, and refrigerate 3 to 5 days. Once cooked it can be refrigerated 1 to 3 days. When cooked, cauliflower has a mild cabbagelike flavor and aroma.

Creamed Collards

prep: 20 min. • cook: 38 min.

4½ lb. fresh collard greens*
1   lb. bacon
¼   cup butter
2   large onions, diced
3   cups chicken broth
½   cup apple cider vinegar
1   tsp. salt
½   tsp. pepper
Béchamel Sauce

1. Rinse collard greens. Trim and discard thick stems from bottom of collard green leaves (about 2 inches); coarsely chop collards.
2. Cook bacon, in batches, in an 8-qt. stockpot over medium heat 10 to 12 minutes or until crisp. Remove bacon and drain on paper towels, reserving drippings in stockpot. Crumble bacon, reserving ¼ cup.
3. Add butter and onions to hot drippings in skillet. Sauté onion 8 minutes or until tender. Add collards, in batches, and cook, stirring occasionally, 5 minutes or until wilted. Stir in chicken broth, next 3 ingredients, and remaining bacon.
4. Bring to a boil. Reduce heat to low, and cook, stirring occasionally, 15 minutes or to desired degree of tenderness. Drain collards, reserving 1 cup liquid.
5. Stir in Béchamel Sauce. Stir in reserved cooking liquid, ¼ cup at a time, to desired consistency. Transfer to a serving dish, and sprinkle with reserved ¼ cup bacon. **Yield:** 8 to 10 servings.

*2 (1-lb.) packages fresh collard greens, thoroughly washed, trimmed, and chopped, may be substituted.

After buying fresh greens, wrap them, unwashed, in damp paper towels, and store in an unsealed plastic bag in the refrigerator for 3 to 5 days.

To clean greens, pull apart the bunch; remove and discard any yellowed or limp leaves. Wash the greens in cool water, agitating with your hands. Replace the water 2 or 3 times, until there are no traces of dirt or grit. Pat dry with paper towels or use a salad spinner. Place on a cutting board, and cut away tough stems. To remove the hard center vein, fold the leaf in half and tear or cut away.

béchamel sauce

prep: 10 min. • cook: 7 min.

½   cup butter
2   medium shallots, minced
2   garlic cloves, pressed
¾   cup all-purpose flour
4   cups milk
½   tsp. salt
½   tsp. pepper
¼   tsp. ground nutmeg

1. Melt butter in a heavy saucepan over low heat; add shallots and garlic, and sauté 1 minute. Whisk in flour until smooth. Cook 1 minute, whisking constantly.
2. Increase heat to medium. Gradually whisk in milk; cook over medium heat, whisking constantly, 5 to 7 minutes or until mixture is thickened and bubbly. Stir in salt, pepper, and nutmeg. **Yield:** about 4½ cups.

Béchamel (bay-shah-MEHL) is the French term for white sauce.

Grilled Sweet Potatoes
With Creamy Basil Vinaigrette

prep: 10 min. • **cook: 24 min.** • **other: 10 min.**

For a fresh twist on one of fall's favorite vegetables, drizzle Creamy Basil Vinaigrette over sweet potato "fries" hot off the grill.

3　lb. sweet potatoes
　　(about 4 to 5)
Vegetable cooking spray
Creamy Basil Vinaigrette

1. Preheat grill to 350° to 400° (medium-high). Bring potatoes and water to cover to a boil in a Dutch oven over high heat; reduce heat to medium-high, and cook 12 to 15 minutes or just until slightly tender. Drain. Plunge potatoes into ice water to stop the cooking process. Drain well. Let stand 10 minutes. Peel and cut into wedges.

2. Coat cold cooking grate with cooking spray, and place on grill over 350° to 400° (medium-high) heat. Place potatoes on cooking grate, and grill, covered with grill lid, 6 to 7 minutes on each side or until grill marks appear. Drizzle potato wedges with Creamy Basil Vinaigrette, and serve immediately. **Yield:** 6 servings.

creamy basil vinaigrette

prep: 10 min.

½　cup plain fat-free yogurt
2　Tbsp. chopped fresh basil
2　Tbsp. balsamic vinaigrette
2　Tbsp. honey
¼　cup red wine vinegar
½　tsp. salt
¼　tsp. pepper

1. Whisk together all ingredients. Serve immediately, or cover and chill up to 8 hours. If chilling, let stand at room temperature 30 minutes before serving. **Yield:** about 1 cup.

note: For testing purposes only, we used Newman's Own Balsamic Vinaigrette.

Roasted Apples and Sweet Potatoes
in Honey-Bourbon Glaze

prep: 32 min.　·　cook: 1 hr., 46 min.　·　other: 45 min.

5　large sweet potatoes
　　(about 5 lb.)
3　Golden Delicious apples
¼　cup fresh lemon juice
⅔　cup firmly packed brown
　　sugar
½　cup honey
6　Tbsp. unsalted butter
¼　cup bourbon
1　tsp. ground cinnamon
½　tsp. ground ginger
½　tsp. salt
⅔　cup coarsely chopped
　　pecans

1. Preheat oven to 400°. Wash sweet potatoes, and place on a baking sheet; prick with a fork. Bake at 400° for 1 hour or until almost tender. Remove from oven. Let stand 45 minutes or until cooled.
2. Meanwhile, peel and core apples. Slice apples into ⅓-inch-thick wedges; toss with lemon juice in a bowl.
3. Peel cooled potatoes, and cut into ⅓-inch-thick slices. Arrange potatoes and apples alternately in a greased 13- x 9-inch baking dish. Pour remaining lemon juice over potatoes and apples.
4. Combine brown sugar and next 6 ingredients in a saucepan, stirring well. Bring to a boil over medium heat, stirring occasionally; boil 2 minutes or until slightly thickened. Pour glaze over potatoes and apples. Bake, uncovered, at 400° for 30 minutes.
5. Remove pan from oven. Baste with glaze in bottom of dish, and sprinkle pecans across top. Bake 14 to 15 more minutes or until apples look roasted. Baste with glaze just before serving. **Yield:** 12 servings.

This oven-roasted side is flavored with a spicy, sweet glaze. Chopped pecans sprinkled across the top add a nice finishing crunch.

tips from the farm

Keeping Sweet Potatoes Fresh sweet potatoes are generally thought of as a fall crop, though they are available year-round. Store sweet potatoes in a cool (around 55°), dry, dark place (do not refrigerate). Under perfect conditions they can be stored for 3 to 4 weeks.

Apple-Walnut Salad

prep: 20 min. • **cook: 8 min.** • **other: 6 hr.**

You can change the flavor of a dish by switching the variety of the apple used. A handy hint: round-bottomed apples are for baking, while those with bumps at the base are eaten out of hand or tossed into salads.

1 cup chopped walnuts, divided
⅔ cup mayonnaise
½ cup lemon curd
¼ tsp. ground cardamom
¼ tsp. ground nutmeg
⅛ tsp. ground cinnamon
1½ tsp. lemon zest, divided
2 Gala apples, chopped
2 Granny Smith apples, chopped
2 Red Delicious apples, chopped
¾ cup thinly sliced celery
1 cup dried fruit mix

1. Preheat oven to 350°. Place walnuts in a single layer in a shallow pan.
2. Bake at 350° for 8 to 10 minutes or until lightly toasted, stirring once after 5 minutes.
3. Stir together mayonnaise, next 4 ingredients, and ½ tsp. lemon zest in a large bowl. Add apples, celery, fruit mix, and ¾ cup walnuts; toss well. Cover and chill 6 hours. Sprinkle with remaining ¼ cup walnuts and 1 tsp. lemon zest. **Yield:** 6 to 8 servings.

note: For testing purposes only, we used Sun-Maid Fruit Bits.

how to cut an apple

1. Pierce the center of the apple with an apple corer and rotate to remove the core. Use a paring knife to slice the apple in half vertically. **2.** Place apple halves cut side down, on a cutting board. Cut through the skin to create apple wedges. **3.** Chop wedges into bite-sized pieces with a paring knife.

Pecan-Beet Salad

prep: 20 min. • cook: 1 hr., 5 min. • other: 30 min.

6   medium-size golden beets
     (about 6 oz. each)
1   cup pecan halves
¼   cup rice wine vinegar
1   large shallot, minced
2   Tbsp. light brown sugar
½   tsp. salt
½   tsp. freshly ground pepper
½   tsp. vanilla extract
¼   cup canola oil
1   (5-oz.) package gourmet
     mixed salad greens,
     thoroughly washed
1   cup (4 oz.) crumbled
     Gorgonzola cheese

1. Preheat oven to 400°. Trim beet stems to 1 inch; gently wash beets. Wrap individually in aluminum foil, and place on a jelly-roll pan.
2. Bake at 400° for 1 hour or until tender. Transfer to a wire rack, and let cool, wrapped in foil, 30 minutes.
3. Meanwhile, decrease oven temperature to 350°. Bake pecans in a single layer in a jelly-roll pan 5 minutes or until toasted and fragrant. Cool completely on wire rack (about 15 minutes).
4. Whisk together vinegar and next 5 ingredients in a small bowl. Add oil in a slow, steady stream, whisking constantly until smooth.
5. Peel beets, and remove stem ends. Cut beets into ½-inch wedges; gently toss with ⅓ cup vinegar mixture.
6. Arrange greens on a serving platter. Top with beet mixture, Gorgonzola cheese, and pecans; serve with remaining vinaigrette. **Yield:** 4 to 6 servings.

Roast golden beets, and you're in for a sweet surprise. Lightly dressed with a brown sugar-and-vanilla vinaigrette, this salad is perfect for a special dinner.

tips from the kitchen

Preparing Beets For this salad, you can roast and peel the beets up to 2 days ahead, and chill them in a zip-top bag. When prepping, don't peel them or trim the little tails on the bottom. Do remove the greens, but leave an inch of the stems to ensure that the pigment remains inside the beets during roasting. Similar in flavor to Swiss chard, beet greens can be prepared in the same way as turnips or collards.

Toasted Pecan-and-Broccoli Salad

prep: 15 min. • **cook: 6 min.** • **other: 2 hr.**

Serve this yummy salad alongside beef or chicken for a sweet and tangy side.

⅓ cup chopped pecans
1 cup light mayonnaise
⅓ cup sugar
2 Tbsp. cider vinegar
1½ lb. fresh broccoli florets, chopped*
¼ cup chopped red onion
⅓ cup sweetened dried cranberries or raisins
4 cooked reduced-fat bacon slices, crumbled

1. Preheat oven to 350°. Place chopped pecans in a single layer in a shallow pan.
2. Bake at 350° for 6 to 8 minutes or until lightly toasted, stirring occasionally.
3. Stir together mayonnaise, sugar, and vinegar in a large bowl; add broccoli, onion, and cranberries, gently tossing to coat. Cover and chill 2 hours. Sprinkle with bacon and pecans just before serving. **Yield:** 10 servings.

*2 (12-oz.) packages fresh broccoli slaw may be substituted.

Broccoli Salad With Lemon Pepper-Blue Cheese Dressing

prep: 20 min. • **cook: 4 min.** • **other: 2 hr.**

½ cup pine nuts
1 (4-oz.) package crumbled blue cheese
½ cup reduced-fat mayonnaise
½ cup reduced-fat sour cream
2 Tbsp. sugar
1 Tbsp. lemon zest
¼ cup fresh lemon juice
2 tsp. freshly ground pepper
¼ tsp. salt
⅛ tsp. ground red pepper
6 cups chopped fresh broccoli (about 1½ lb.)
1½ cups chopped Gala apple (1 large apple)
¾ cup dried cherries

1. Heat pine nuts in a small nonstick skillet over medium-low heat, stirring often, 4 to 5 minutes or until toasted and fragrant.
2. Whisk together blue cheese crumbles and next 8 ingredients in a large bowl; add broccoli, apple, and cherries, gently tossing to coat. Cover and chill 2 to 8 hours; stir in toasted pine nuts just before serving. **Yield:** 8 servings.

Toasted Pecan-and-Broccoli Salad

Autumn Salad With Maple-Cider Vinaigrette

prep: 10 min.

1 (10-oz.) bag baby spinach
1 ripe Bartlett pear, cored and thinly sliced
1 small red onion, thinly sliced
1 (4-oz.) package crumbled blue cheese
Sugared Curried Walnuts
Maple-Cider Vinaigrette

1. Combine first 5 ingredients in a large bowl. Drizzle with Maple-Cider Vinaigrette, gently tossing to coat. **Yield:** 8 servings.

Place a pear in a paper sack to speed ripening. Once ripened, fresh pears will keep for several days in the refrigerator. Don't store in plastic bags. The dressing and nuts for this recipe can be made ahead.

sugared curried walnuts

prep: 5 min. • **cook:** 10 min.

1 (6-oz.) package walnut halves
2 Tbsp. butter, melted
3 Tbsp. sugar
¼ tsp. ground ginger
⅛ tsp. curry powder
⅛ tsp. kosher salt
⅛ tsp. ground red pepper

1. Preheat oven to 350°. Toss walnuts in melted butter. Stir together sugar and next 4 ingredients in a medium bowl; sprinkle over walnuts, tossing to coat. Spread in a single layer on a nonstick aluminum foil-lined pan.
2. Bake at 350° for 10 minutes. Cool in pan on a wire rack; separate walnuts with a fork. Store in an airtight container for up to 1 week. **Yield:** 1½ cups.

maple-cider vinaigrette

prep: 5 min.

1⅓ cup cider vinegar
2 Tbsp. pure maple syrup
1 Tbsp. Dijon mustard
¼ tsp. salt
¼ tsp. pepper
⅔ cup olive oil

1. Whisk together first 5 ingredients. Gradually whisk in oil until completely blended. Cover and refrigerate up to 3 days. **Yield:** 1⅓ cups.

Pumpkin-Pecan Layer Cake

prep: 30 min. • **cook: 18 min.** • **other: 1 hr., 10 min.**

To roast fresh pumpkin, microwave a pie pumpkin on HIGH 2 minutes. Carefully cut pumpkin in half using a sharp knife. Scoop out seeds and stringy pulp. Place cut sides down in a 13- x 9-inch pan. Add ¼- to ½-inch water. Cover and roast at 375° for 50 to 60 minutes or until very tender. Cool and scoop out pulp. Use pumpkin as directed in recipe.

½ cup butter, softened
1½ cups firmly packed light
    brown sugar
2 large eggs
1 cup fresh (see blurb at left)
    or canned pumpkin
2 cups all-purpose flour
2 tsp. baking powder
2 tsp. pumpkin pie spice
½ tsp. baking soda
½ tsp. salt
½ cup buttermilk
2 tsp. vanilla extract
2 tsp. minced fresh ginger
1 cup chopped pecans, toasted
Ginger–Cream Cheese Frosting

1. Preheat oven to 350°. Beat butter and brown sugar at medium speed with an electric mixer until light and fluffy. Add eggs, 1 at a time, beating until blended after each addition. Add pumpkin, beating until blended.

2. Combine flour and next 4 ingredients. Combine buttermilk, vanilla, and ginger. Add flour mixture to butter mixture alternately with gingered buttermilk, beginning and ending with flour mixture. Beat at low speed after each addition. Fold in chopped pecans. Pour batter into 2 greased, parchment paper-lined 9-inch round cake pans.

3. Bake at 350° for 18 to 20 minutes or until a wooden pick inserted in center comes out clean. Let cool in pans on wire racks 10 minutes. Remove from pans to wire racks, and cool completely (about 1 hour).

4. Spread Ginger–Cream Cheese Frosting between layers and on top and sides of cake. Cover and chill overnight. **Yield:** 8 servings.

ginger–cream cheese frosting

prep: 7 min. • **other: 30 min.**

1½ (8-oz.) packages cream
    cheese, softened
½ cup butter, softened
1 Tbsp. minced fresh ginger
4 cups powdered sugar
1 tsp. vanilla extract

1. Beat first 3 ingredients at medium speed with an electric mixer until light and fluffy. Gradually add powdered sugar, beating until smooth. Add vanilla, beating until smooth. Chill 30 minutes or until spreading consistency. **Yield:** 2¼ cups.

Caramel-Glazed Pear Cake

prep: 25 min. • **cook:** 1 hr.

4   ripe Bartlett pears, peeled
    and diced (about 3 cups)
1   Tbsp. sugar
3   large eggs
2   cups sugar
1¼ cups vegetable oil
3   cups all-purpose flour
1   tsp. salt
1   tsp. baking soda
1½ cups pecans, coarsely
    chopped
2   tsp. vanilla extract
Caramel Glaze

1. Preheat oven to 350°. Toss together pears and 1 Tbsp. sugar; let stand 5 minutes.
2. Beat eggs, 2 cups sugar, and oil at medium speed with an electric mixer until blended.
3. Combine flour, salt, and baking soda, and add to egg mixture, beating at low speed until blended. Fold in pears, chopped pecans, and vanilla extract. Pour batter into a greased and floured 10-inch Bundt pan.
4. Bake at 350° for 1 hour or until a wooden pick inserted in center of cake comes out clean. Remove from pan, and drizzle Caramel Glaze over warm cake. **Yield:** 12 servings.

Pecans and a brown sugar glaze give this cake a decidedly Southern accent. Use very ripe pears to make the cake ultra-moist.

caramel glaze

prep: 5 min. • **cook:** 8 min.

1   cup brown sugar
½   cup butter
¼   cup evaporated milk

1. Stir together brown sugar, butter, and evaporated milk in a small saucepan over medium heat; bring to a boil, and cook, stirring constantly, 2½ minutes or until sugar dissolves. **Yield:** 1½ cups.

tips from the farm

Picking Pears Pears don't ripen well on trees; they're picked when mature, but not ripe. You'll know when a pear is ripe by applying gentle pressure at the base of the stem. If it yields slightly to pressure, it's ripe.

Cranberry Upside-Down Cake

prep: 16 min. • **cook: 55 min.** • **other: 10 min.**

Shiny glazed cranberries give a tangy new twist to this classic homestyle dessert.

½ cup butter
3 Tbsp. amaretto liqueur
1¼ cups firmly packed brown sugar
24 whole natural almonds, lightly toasted
2¼ cups fresh or frozen cranberries
¾ cup coarsely chopped natural almonds, toasted
1½ cups all-purpose flour
2 tsp. baking powder
½ cup butter, softened
1 cup granulated sugar
3 large eggs
½ cup milk
1 Tbsp. vanilla extract
1 tsp. almond extract

1. Preheat oven to 350°. Melt ½ cup butter in a lightly greased 10-inch cast-iron skillet over low heat. Stir amaretto into melted butter; sprinkle brown sugar into skillet. Remove from heat.

2. Arrange whole almonds around edge of skillet. Sprinkle cranberries and chopped almonds over brown sugar.

3. Whisk together flour and baking powder in a medium bowl. Set aside. Beat softened butter at medium speed with an electric mixer until creamy; gradually add granulated sugar, beating well. Add eggs, 1 at a time, beating until blended after each addition. Add flour mixture to butter mixture, alternately with milk, beginning and ending with flour mixture. Beat at low speed until blended after each addition. Stir in extracts. Pour batter over cranberries and almonds in skillet.

4. Bake at 350° for 55 to 60 minutes or until a wooden pick inserted in center comes out clean. Let cool in skillet on a wire rack 10 minutes. Run a knife around edges. Invert cake onto a serving plate. **Yield:** 8 servings.

tips from our kitchen

Craving Cranberries Fresh cranberries will keep in the refrigerator up to 4 weeks. They also can be frozen up to 9 months; it's not necessary to thaw frozen berries before using them in baked goods.

Star Pecan Pie

prep: 18 min.   •   **cook:** 50 min.

Classic Pastry Shell and Pastry
   Stars
4   large eggs
1   Tbsp. whipping cream
1   cup firmly packed dark brown
   sugar
¾   cup light corn syrup
6   Tbsp. unsalted butter, melted
2   tsp. vanilla extract
¼   tsp. salt
1½ cups chopped pecans,
   lightly toasted
⅔   cup pecan halves

1. Preheat oven to 350°. Prepare dough for Classic Pastry Shell and Pastry Stars. Roll three-fourths of dough to ⅛-inch thickness on a lightly floured surface. Place in a 9-inch pie plate, trim off excess pastry along edges. Fold edges under, and crimp. Place pastry in refrigerator while preparing Pastry Stars and pie filling.

2. Line a baking sheet with parchment paper. Roll remaining dough to ⅛-inch thickness on a lightly floured surface. Using a 1-inch star-shaped cutter, cut out 12 stars. Repeat procedure using a 1½-inch star-shaped cutter to cut out 5 stars. Transfer stars to prepared baking sheet. Whisk together 1 egg and cream in a small bowl. Remove pastry from refrigerator. Brush egg wash over Pastry Stars and around crimped edge of pastry.

3. Whisk remaining 3 eggs in a bowl. Whisk in brown sugar and next 4 ingredients; stir in chopped pecans. Pour filling into pastry shell. Arrange pecan halves around outer edge of filling. Arrange Pastry Stars on top of pie.

4. Bake at 350° on bottom oven rack for 50 to 55 minutes or until filling is set and pastry stars are browned. Transfer to a wire rack to cool completely. **Yield:** 8 servings.

As a timesaver, omit the Classic Pastry recipe and use 1 (15-oz.) package refrigerated piecrusts. Unroll 1 piecrust and place in a 9-inch pie plate. Fold edges under, and crimp. Unroll the remaining piecrust and cut out stars according to the recipe. Prepare the pie and filling as directed.

classic pastry shell and pastry stars

prep: 7 min.

2   cups all-purpose flour
1   tsp. salt
¾   cup chilled shortening
5   to 6 Tbsp. ice water

1. Whisk together flour and salt; cut in shortening with a pastry blender until mixture is the size of peas. Sprinkle ice water, 1 Tbsp. at a time, over surface; stir with a fork until dry ingredients are moistened. Shape into a ball. **Yield:** enough pastry for 1 (9-inch) pie.

Triple Nut Tart

prep: 15 min. • **cook: 1 hr., 5 min.**

Three types of nuts crown this tart that's reminiscent of pecan pie in flavor.

½ (15-oz.) package refrigerated piecrusts
1 cup sugar
½ cup light corn syrup
¼ cup butter
4 large eggs, lightly beaten
1 tsp. vanilla extract
¼ tsp. salt
½ cup pecan halves
½ cup macadamia nuts
⅓ cup blanched whole almonds, toasted

1. Preheat oven to 400°. Unroll piecrust, and fit piecrust into a greased and floured 9½-inch round tart pan with a removable bottom. Prick bottom of piecrust with a fork.
2. Bake at 400° for 10 minutes or until golden. Cool on a wire rack. Reduce oven temperature to 325°.
3. Stir together sugar, corn syrup, and butter in a saucepan; cook over medium heat until butter melts and sugar dissolves, stirring often. Remove from heat; cool slightly. Add eggs, vanilla, and salt; stir well. Stir in nuts. Spoon filling into crust.
4. Bake at 325° for 55 minutes or until set. Cool on a wire rack. **Yield:** 8 servings.

tips from the farm

Nut Basics Because they contain high amounts of oil, nuts can go rancid and develop a stale taste fairly quickly. Unshelled nuts will keep well up to 6 months if stored in a cool, dark, dry place. If shelled, nuts can be kept in an airtight container in the refrigerator up to a year or in the freezer for 2 years or longer. Vacuum-packed nuts can be stored at room temperature.

Cinnamon-Caramel Apple Dumplings With Golden Raisins

prep: 30 min. · cook: 20 min.

1 (15-oz.) package refrigerated piecrusts
6 large Rome or Granny Smith apples, cored
6 Tbsp. golden raisins
1 large egg, beaten
½ cup butter, melted
1 cup firmly packed light brown sugar
¼ cup corn syrup
½ cup apple juice
1 tsp. ground cinnamon
6 cinnamon sticks

1. Preheat oven to 425°. Unroll piecrusts onto a lightly floured surface; cut dough into 12 (10- x 1¼-inch) strips, reserving dough scraps for later use. Crisscross 2 strips of dough on surface, forming an "X." Place 1 apple in center of "X." Spoon 1 Tbsp. raisins into apple core, pressing raisins to compact. Pull strips up and over apple, pressing dough into core; trim off excess, if necessary. Repeat with remaining piecrust strips, apples, and raisins.

2. Stir together egg and 1 Tbsp. water; brush dough strips on apples with egg mixture.

3. Whisk together melted butter and next 4 ingredients; pour mixture into a 13- x 9-inch baking dish. Place apples in baking dish.

4. Bake at 425° for 20 to 25 minutes or until pastry is golden brown, shielding apple tops with aluminum foil after 15 minutes to prevent excessive browning, if necessary. Remove from oven. Press 1 cinnamon stick into center of each apple to resemble a stem. Drizzle sauce in pan over apples. Garnish, if desired. **Yield:** 6 servings.

tips from our kitchen

All About Apples You can change the flavor of a dish simply by switching the variety of the apple used. A handy hint to remember: Round-bottomed apples are better suited for baking, while those with bumps at the base are eaten out of hand or tossed in salads. When shopping, look for apples that are free from bruises, feel firm to a light squeeze, and are deeply colored. Store them in the produce drawer of the refrigerator, and they'll stay fresh for a week.

winter storehouse

Butternut Squash Spread on Cheese Croutons

prep: 22 min. • cook: 1 hr., 7 min.

Baked butternut squash and Asiago cheese blend with herbs and toasted pecans for a fabulous-tasting spread.

1   medium butternut squash
3   Tbsp. butter, melted
3   garlic cloves, minced
½   (8-oz.) package cream cheese, softened
1½ cups freshly grated Asiago cheese, divided
1   Tbsp. sugar
½   cup chopped pecans, toasted
2   tsp. chopped fresh thyme
2   tsp. chopped fresh rosemary
1   baguette, cut into 48 thin slices
½   cup olive oil
Salt and pepper
Garnishes: small sprigs of fresh thyme and rosemary

1. Preheat oven to 350°. Microwave squash on HIGH 1 to 2 minutes. (This step softens squash for slicing.) Cut squash in half lengthwise; remove and discard seeds. Place squash, cut side down, in a 13- x 9-inch baking dish. Add hot water to dish to depth of 1 inch. Bake, uncovered, at 350° for 1 hour or until squash is tender.

2. Scoop out squash pulp. Mash pulp, and place in a large bowl.

3. Melt butter in a small skillet over medium-high heat. Add garlic; sauté 1 minute. Add garlic butter to squash pulp in bowl. Add cream cheese, ½ cup Asiago cheese, and sugar; beat at medium speed with an electric mixer until smooth. Stir in pecans and chopped herbs.

4. Place baguette slices on 2 large ungreased baking sheets; brush or drizzle olive oil over baguette slices. Sprinkle with salt and pepper. Increase oven temperature to 400°, and bake for 4 minutes. Sprinkle baguette slices with remaining 1 cup Asiago cheese. Bake 2 more minutes or until cheese melts.

5. Spoon 1 Tbsp. squash mixture onto each cheese crouton. Garnish, if desired. **Yield:** 4 dozen.

Caramelized Onion-Cranberry Compote

prep: 10 min. • cook: 17 min.

1 Tbsp. butter

2 cups thinly sliced sweet onions

¼ cup balsamic vinegar

½ cup fresh or frozen cranberries (thawed), coarsely chopped

1 Tbsp. sugar

½ tsp. salt

½ tsp. orange zest

1. Melt butter in a large skillet over medium heat; add onions, and sauté 15 to 18 minutes or until golden and tender. Stir in vinegar and remaining ingredients; cook, stirring occasionally, 2 to 4 minutes or until liquid is reduced to about 2 Tbsp. **Yield:** 1 cup.

Caramelized Onion-Cranberry–Cream Cheese Bites: Spread 16 whole grain crackers each with 1½ tsp. ⅓-less-fat cream cheese; top each with 1 Tbsp. Caramelized Onion-Cranberry Compote. Garnish with fresh cilantro or parsley leaves.

You can make this a day ahead and store it in an air tight container in the fridge. Let stand at room temperature 30 minutes before serving.

Herbed Nuts

Herbed Nuts

prep: 7 min. • **cook: 20 min.**

2   cups pecan halves
2   cups cashews
⅓   cup butter, melted
2   Tbsp. minced fresh rosemary
1   Tbsp. chopped fresh thyme
1   tsp. salt
½   tsp. ground sage
½   tsp. ground red pepper

1. Preheat oven to 350°. Combine all ingredients in a large bowl; stir well. Spread nuts on an ungreased jelly-roll pan. Bake at 350° for 20 to 25 minutes, stirring every 10 minutes. Cool completely in pan. Store in an airtight container. **Yield:** 4½ cups.

Turn these nuts into a toasty snack with just a few minutes of baking and some fresh herbs. Serve them when guests come for dinner.

Herb-and-Cheese Coins

prep: 15 min. • **cook: 12 min.** • **other: 2 hr.**

2   (4-oz.) packages crumbled blue cheese, softened
½   cup butter, softened
1⅓ cups all-purpose flour
⅓   cup toasted, ground walnuts
1   egg white, beaten
Tiny fresh herb sprigs (such as rosemary, thyme, and sage)

1. Preheat oven to 350°. Beat cheese and butter at medium speed with an electric mixer until creamy. Add flour and nuts; beat until blended.
2. Shape dough into 2 (8-inch) logs. Wrap logs in wax paper, and chill 2 hours or until firm.
3. Cut into ¼-inch-thick slices, and place on lightly greased baking sheets. Brush lightly with beaten egg white. Press herb sprigs firmly into each slice.
4. Bake at 350° for 12 to 15 minutes or until golden. Cool 1 minute on baking sheets; remove to wire racks to cool completely. **Yield:** 4 dozen.

Walnuts and blue cheese blend deliciously in these little savory cookies. Pour your favorite wine, and welcome your friends over.

tips from our kitchen

Chop Fresh Herbs With Ease Here's an easy way to chop fresh herbs: stuff the leaves into a glass measuring cup and insert kitchen shears or scissors; snip in cup, rotating shears with each snip.

Sweet Potato Squares With Lemon-Garlic Mayonnaise

prep: 30 min. • cook: 18 min.

2 lb. sweet potatoes, peeled and cut into 32 (1-inch) cubes
2 Tbsp. olive oil
½ tsp. pepper
¼ tsp. salt
½ lb. spicy smoked sausage, cut into 32 (½-inch) pieces
32 wooden picks
Lemon-Garlic Mayonnaise
Garnish: fresh thyme sprigs

1. Preheat oven to 450°. Place sweet potato cubes on a lightly greased 15- x 10-inch jelly-roll pan. Drizzle potatoes with 2 Tbsp. oil, and sprinkle with pepper and salt. Toss to coat.
2. Bake at 450° for 15 to 20 minutes, turning cubes twice.
3. Cook sausage in a large nonstick skillet over medium-high heat 3 to 4 minutes on each side or until browned. Drain on paper towels.
4. Place 1 sausage slice on top of 1 sweet potato cube; secure with a wooden pick. Repeat with remaining sausage slices and potato cubes. Serve with Lemon-Garlic Mayonnaise. Garnish, if desired. **Yield**: 8 appetizer servings.

lemon-garlic mayonnaise

prep: 10 min.

1 cup mayonnaise
2 Tbsp. chopped fresh flat-leaf parsley
2 tsp. minced garlic
1 tsp. lemon zest
2 Tbsp. fresh lemon juice
½ tsp. pepper
¼ tsp. salt

1. Stir together all ingredients. Store in an airtight container in refrigerator up to 7 days. **Yield:** about 1 cup.

Creamy Lemon-Garlic Dressing: Stir together ⅓ cup Lemon-Garlic Mayonnaise, ¼ cup buttermilk, and a pinch of salt. **Yield:** about ½ cup.

Carolyn's Earth Art
Working God's Garden

Carolyn M. Wood
owner

The Farm House Resturant
469 Farmhouse Road
Ellerslie, Ga. 31807
(706) 329-1037

whosalliesue@yahoo.com

Pineapple Wassail

Pineapple Wassail

prep: 5 min. • **cook: 20 min.**

4   cups unsweetened pineapple
    juice
1   (12-oz.) can apricot nectar
2   cups apple cider
1   cup orange juice
1   tsp. whole cloves
3   (6-inch) cinnamon sticks,
    broken
Garnishes: orange wedges,
    whole cinnamon sticks

1. Bring first 6 ingredients to a boil in a Dutch oven; reduce heat, and simmer 20 minutes. Pour through a wire-mesh strainer, discarding spices. Serve hot. Garnish, if desired. **Yield:** 2 qt.

Not only will this beverage warm you on a brisk winter's day, it will also fill your kitchen with the spicy fragrances of cinnamon and cloves.

Belgian Wassail

prep: 15 min. • **cook: 25 min.**

2   oranges
2   lemons
1   gal. apple cider
1   cup sugar
2   (3-inch) cinnamon sticks
1   tsp. whole allspice

1. Squeeze juice from oranges and lemons into a bowl, reserving rinds.
2. Bring citrus juice, rinds, apple cider, and next 3 ingredients to a boil over medium-high heat. Reduce heat, and simmer 25 minutes. Pour mixture through a wire-mesh strainer into a container, discarding solids. **Yield:** about 1 gal.

Ginger Beer

prep: 10 min. • **other: 4 hr.**

1   qt. water
1   cup sugar
⅓   cup grated fresh ginger
1½   tsp. lime zest
2   Tbsp. fresh lime juice

1. Combine all ingredients, stirring until sugar dissolves. Cover and chill 4 hours.
2. Pour ginger mixture through a wire-mesh strainer into a large pitcher, discarding solids. Serve over crushed ice. **Yield:** 5 cups.

Bourbon Sunrise

prep: 15 min. • **cook:** 10 min.

Fresh-squeezed juice from sliced navel oranges gives this beverage a burst of flavor.

½ cup water
1 cup sugar
2 large navel oranges, sliced
1½ cups bourbon
1 qt. orange juice
1 (10-oz.) jar maraschino cherries with stems, undrained

1. Combine ½ cup water, sugar, and orange juices in a saucepan, squeezing slices to release juices. Bring to a boil; cook over medium-high heat, stirring often, 5 minutes. Cover; remove from heat. Cool.
2. Pour syrup through a wire-mesh strainer into a pitcher, discarding orange slices; stir in bourbon and orange juice. Stir in cherry juice and cherries. Serve over ice. **Yield:** 8½ cups.

Grapefruit-Rosemary Daiquiris

prep: 17 min. • **cook:** 10 min. • **other:** 8 hr.

The surprising combo of citrus and herb tastes great in this slushy daiquiri. For a special effect, dip rims of glasses in coarse sugar before filling.

3 cups (about 7 grapefruit) freshly squeezed ruby red grapefruit juice*
⅔ cup sugar
2 large sprigs fresh rosemary
⅓ cup vodka (optional)
1½ tsp. finely chopped fresh rosemary
Sparkling white sugar (optional)
Garnish: fresh rosemary sprigs

1. Pour 2½ cups grapefruit juice into 2 ice cube trays; freeze until firm. Cover and chill remaining juice.
2. Stir together 1½ cups water, sugar, and 2 rosemary sprigs in a saucepan; bring to a boil. Cover, reduce heat, and simmer 10 minutes. Remove from heat; discard rosemary sprigs. Cool syrup; chill.
3. Process frozen juice cubes, remaining ½ cup grapefruit juice, rosemary syrup, vodka, if desired, and chopped rosemary in a 5-cup blender for 10 seconds or until slushy. Serve in sugar-rimmed glasses, and garnish, if desired. **Yield:** 5 cups.

*Bottled ruby red grapefruit juice may be substituted.

note: For sugared rims, dip rims of stemmed glasses into a thin coating of light corn syrup or water, and then spin rims in a plateful of sparkling white sugar.

Bourbon Sunrise

Peppered Pork Tenderloin With Roasted Fennel

prep: 7 min. · cook: 31 min.

Use a sharp boning knife to trim tough silver skin from pork tenderloin before baking it.

2   fennel bulbs
3   large portobello mushroom caps
1   (2-lb.) package pork tenderloins, trimmed
¼   cup olive oil, divided
2   Tbsp. coarsely ground black peppercorns, divided
½   tsp. salt
½   cup dry sherry
1   cup whipping cream

1. Preheat oven to 425°. Trim base from fennel bulbs; cut bulbs into sixths, discarding fronds. Cut mushroom caps into fourths. Set aside.
2. Brown tenderloins in 2 Tbsp. hot oil in a large skillet over medium-high heat 4 minutes on each side. Place pork in a shallow roasting pan; sprinkle with 1 Tbsp. pepper and ½ tsp. salt. Arrange fennel and mushrooms around tenderloins; drizzle with remaining 2 Tbsp. oil.
3. Bake at 425° for 20 minutes or until a meat thermometer inserted in thickest portion registers 155°. Transfer tenderloins to a serving platter; let stand, covered, 5 minutes or until thermometer registers 160°.
4. Place roasting pan over 2 burners of cooktop; add sherry, stirring with a whisk to loosen any browned bits from bottom of pan. Whisk in whipping cream and remaining 1 Tbsp. pepper; bring to a boil. Cook, whisking constantly, 3 to 4 minutes or until sauce is slightly thickened. Serve over sliced tenderloin and vegetables. **Yield:** 4 servings.

tips from the farm

Fresh Fennel When raw, fennel is licorice flavored and has a crisp texture. When cooked, its flavor becomes more delicate and the texture softens. Store fresh fennel in a plastic bag in the refrigerator up to 5 days.

Pasta-and-Greens Torte

prep: 12 min. • **cook: 28 min.** • **other: 10 min.**

1 lb. fresh Swiss chard
8 large eggs
1 cup milk
1 cup ricotta cheese
1½ tsp. dried thyme
1½ tsp. salt
½ tsp. pepper
1 (9-oz.) package refrigerated linguine, cut in half
3 Tbsp. olive oil
2 cups (8 oz.) shredded Italian blend cheese

1. Preheat oven to 400°. Bring 4 qt. water to a boil in a 6-qt. Dutch oven.

2. While water comes to a boil, remove and discard stems and ribs from chard. Coarsely chop leaves. Wash chard thoroughly in cold water; drain well. Process eggs and next 5 ingredients in a blender until smooth; set aside.

3. Add chard leaves and pasta to boiling water. Return water to a boil; boil 1 minute. Drain well, pressing out excess moisture from chard with the back of a spoon. Return pasta and greens to pan; toss until blended.

4. Brush a 10-inch cast-iron skillet with olive oil. Arrange pasta and greens in skillet; sprinkle with cheese. Pour egg mixture over cheese, pressing to submerge pasta and greens in liquid.

5. Place skillet over medium heat for 2 minutes. Immediately transfer to hot oven. Bake at 400° for 25 minutes or until golden and set. Let stand 10 minutes before inverting onto a serving platter, if desired, and cutting into wedges. **Yield:** 6 to 8 servings.

A well-seasoned cast-iron skillet is in order for this impressive deep-dish entrée.

Roasted Vegetable Lasagna

prep: 34 min. • cook: 1 hr., 38 min. • other: 15 min.

This white-sauced meatless lasagna will appeal to any crowd, vegetarian or not.

1   medium butternut squash (about 2 lb.)
1   small sweet potato, cut into ½-inch cubes (about 1 cup)
3   Tbsp. olive oil, divided
3   cups sliced leeks (about 5 medium)
1   red bell pepper, cut into thin strips
4   cups milk
4   garlic cloves, halved
3   Tbsp. butter
¼   cup all-purpose flour
1   tsp. salt
½   tsp. pepper
9   dried precooked lasagna noodles
1   cup grated Asiago cheese
1   cup whipping cream
½   cup grated Parmesan cheese

1. Preheat oven to 450°. Microwave squash at HIGH 2 minutes. Cut squash in half lengthwise; remove and discard seeds. Peel squash, and cut into ½-inch cubes. Set aside 3 cups cubed squash; reserve any remaining squash for another use. Combine squash, sweet potato, and 2 Tbsp. olive oil on a large rimmed baking sheet. Bake at 450° for 10 minutes.

2. Meanwhile, combine leeks, bell pepper, and remaining 1 Tbsp. oil in a large bowl. Add to partially roasted squash mixture, stirring gently. Bake at 450° for 20 minutes or until tender, stirring after 15 minutes. Return roasted vegetables to bowl; set aside.

3. Combine milk and garlic in a large saucepan; bring just to a boil. Reduce heat, and simmer, uncovered, 10 minutes. Remove and discard garlic.

4. Melt butter in a large saucepan over medium heat; whisk in flour until smooth. Cook 1 minute, whisking constantly. Gradually whisk in warm milk; cook over medium-high heat, whisking constantly, 12 to 13 minutes or until slightly thickened. Remove from heat; stir in salt and pepper. Add to roasted vegetables, stirring gently.

5. Spoon 1 cup vegetable mixture into a lightly greased 13- x 9-inch baking dish. Top with 3 lasagna noodles; spread half of remaining vegetable mixture over noodles, and sprinkle with ½ cup Asiago cheese. Repeat procedure with 3 noodles, remaining vegetable mixture, and remaining Asiago cheese. Break remaining 3 noodles in half and lay on top of casserole.

6. Decrease oven temperature to 350°. Beat cream at high speed with an electric mixer until soft peaks form. Spread whipped cream over noodles; sprinkle with Parmesan cheese. Cover and bake at 350° for 30 minutes. Uncover and bake 13 more minutes or until golden and bubbly. Let stand 15 minutes before serving. **Yield:** 8 servings.

Whole Acorn Squash
Cream Soup

Whole Acorn Squash Cream Soup

prep: 16 min. • **cook: 1 hr., 45 min.**

4 medium acorn squash
¼ cup cream cheese
1 cup heavy whipping cream
1 cup chicken broth
½ tsp. salt
1 tsp. ground cinnamon

1. Preheat oven to 350°. Cut off about 1 inch of stem ends of squash to reveal seeds. Scoop out and discard seeds and membranes. Arrange squash in a 13 x 19 inch baking dish.
2. Place 1 Tbsp. cream cheese in each squash cavity. Pour ¼ cup each heavy cream and chicken broth over cheese in each squash, and sprinkle each cavity with ⅛ tsp. salt and ¼ tsp. cinnamon. Add water to baking dish to a depth of ½ inch.
3. Bake squash, uncovered, at 350° for 1 hour and 45 minutes or until squash are very tender.
4. To serve, carefully set each squash in a shallow soup bowl. **Yield:** 4 servings.

This unique recipe celebrates the beauty of squash by using it as a serving vessel. Choose squash that stand upright for ease in baking and serving. Select firm, unblemished squash that feel heavy for their size. Cut squash will keep in the refrigerator for about 1 week; uncut can be kept for 1 month in a cool, dark place.

Baked Potato Soup

prep: 30 min. • **cook: 30 min.**

5 large baking potatoes, baked
¼ cup butter
1 medium onion, chopped
⅓ cup all-purpose flour
1 qt. half-and-half
3 cups milk
1 tsp. salt
⅛ tsp. pepper
2 cups (8 oz.) shredded Cheddar cheese
8 bacon slices, cooked and crumbled

1. Peel potatoes; coarsely mash with a fork.
2. Melt butter in a Dutch oven over medium heat; add onion, and sauté until tender. Add flour, stirring until smooth.
3. Stir in potatoes, half-and-half, and next 3 ingredients; cook over low heat until thoroughly heated. Top each serving with cheese and bacon. **Yield:** 8 servings.

To bake 5 large potatoes in the microwave, prick each several times with a fork. Microwave 1 inch apart on paper towels at HIGH 14 minutes or until done, turning and rearranging after 5 minutes. Let cool.

Sweet Potato Stew With Red Beans

prep: 22 min. • cook: 7 hr.

A squeeze of lime juice brightens the rich, earthy flavors of this stew.

2   (10 oz.) cans diced tomatoes and mild green chiles
1   (16-oz.) can red beans, rinsed and drained
1   (14-oz.) can vegetable broth
4   cups cubed peeled sweet potato (about 1½ lb.)
1   medium onion, chopped
1   small red bell pepper, chopped
1   garlic clove, minced
1   tsp. grated fresh ginger
½   tsp. salt
½   tsp. ground cumin
¼   tsp. black pepper
3   Tbsp. creamy peanut butter
Chopped dry-roasted peanuts
Lime wedges (optional)

1. Combine first 11 ingredients and ½ cup water in a 5-qt. slow cooker.
2. Cover and cook on LOW 7 hours or until vegetables are tender.
3. Spoon ½ cup cooking liquid into a small bowl. Add peanut butter to liquid, and stir well with a wire whisk. Stir peanut butter mixture into stew. Sprinkle each serving with peanuts. Serve with lime wedges, if desired. **Yield:** 4 to 6 servings.

note: For testing purposes only, we used Rotel Mild diced tomatoes and Bush's red beans.

tips from our kitchen

Best Beans Red beans are different from kidney beans. They are smaller and rounder, like pinto beans, but red in color.

Rob and Megan Weary,
Organic Farmers

Roundabout Farm, Keswick, Virginia

Husband-and-wife and owners of Roundabout Farm, Rob and Megan Weary spend their days at work growing organic herbs, flowers, and vegetables on a former vineyard in the foothills of the Blue Ridge Mountains in Keswick, Virginia.

After living in Italy and the Virgin Islands for a post-college stint, the couple (both University of Virginia grads) decided to move back home to Virginia. "We knew that we always wanted to be here," Megan says.

The Wearys grow dozens of varieties of produce at their farm, but what's unique about Roundabout is the flower operation and the marketing savvy Megan brings to it.

Sunflowers are best-sellers, and their summer zinnias, bundled in tissue paper and tied with grosgrain ribbon, add a refreshing splash of color on the farm. "When people walk away with those wrapped flowers, they feel like movie stars—they feel special," says Megan. "It's incredibly rewarding to provide something that is good, solid, and strong in a place we really love."

Apple-Turnip Mashed Potatoes

prep: 20 min.　·　cook: 26 min.

1　lb. turnips, peeled and cut into 1-inch pieces
1　lb. Yukon gold potatoes, peeled and cut into 1-inch pieces
3　bacon slices, cut into ¼-inch pieces
2　medium-size Golden Delicious apples, peeled and chopped
¼　cup Roasted Garlic*
1　tsp. chopped fresh thyme
¾　cup buttermilk
2　Tbsp. butter, melted
Salt and pepper to taste

1. Bring turnips, potatoes, and salted water to cover to a boil in a Dutch oven; cook 15 to 20 minutes or until tender. Drain.
2. Cook bacon in a medium nonstick skillet over medium-high heat 5 to 6 minutes or until crisp; remove bacon, reserving 2 Tbsp. drippings in skillet. Crumble bacon. Sauté apples in hot drippings in skillet 6 minutes or until tender and lightly browned.
3. Combine apples, turnips, potatoes, Roasted Garlic, and thyme in a bowl; mash with a potato masher until blended. (Mixture will be chunky.) Stir in buttermilk and butter. Season with salt and pepper to taste. Transfer to a bowl.
4. Serve immediately, or, if desired, microwave mixture at HIGH 1 to 2 minutes or until thoroughly heated, stirring at 1-minute intervals. Sprinkle with bacon just before serving. **Yield:** about 8 servings.

*2 tsp. jarred roasted minced garlic may be substituted. Proceed with recipe as directed, sautéing garlic with apples in Step 2.

This rustic and delicious recipe has a chunky consistency.

roasted garlic

prep: 10 min.　·　cook: 30 min.　·　other: 15 min.

4　garlic bulbs
2　Tbsp. olive oil
¼　tsp. kosher salt

1. Preheat oven to 425°. Cut off pointed end of each garlic bulb; place bulbs on a piece of aluminum foil. Drizzle with oil, and sprinkle with salt. Fold foil to seal.
2. Bake at 425° for 30 to 35 minutes; let cool 15 minutes. Squeeze pulp from garlic cloves into a small bowl. Store in an airtight container in the refrigerator up to 3 days. **Yield:** ½ cup.

Perfectly roasted garlic also tastes great spread on toasted French bread or a grilled steak.

Braised Fennel and Leeks

prep: 20 min. • cook: 1 hr., 30 min. • other: 10 min.

Thinly sliced fennel and leeks simmer in a white wine broth and get an herbed crumb topping. Match this side with a pork roast, chicken, or fish.

3   medium fennel bulbs
5   medium leeks, white and light green parts only, halved lengthwise and thinly sliced
1   (14-oz.) can chicken broth
⅓   cup dry white wine
2   Tbsp. chopped fresh parsley
1   tsp. chopped fresh thyme
¾   tsp. salt
¾   tsp. pepper
¼   cup butter, cut into pieces
Heavy-duty aluminum foil
2   cups fresh breadcrumbs
¼   cup olive oil
2   Tbsp. chopped fresh thyme

1. Preheat oven to 400°. Rinse fennel thoroughly. Trim and discard root ends of fennel bulbs. Trim stalks from bulbs, reserving fronds for another use. Cut bulbs into thin slices. Arrange fennel and leeks in a lightly greased 13- x 9-inch baking dish.

2. Combine chicken broth and next 5 ingredients, and pour over vegetables. Dot with butter, and cover tightly with heavy-duty aluminum foil. Bake at 400° for 1 hour.

3. Meanwhile, combine breadcrumbs, olive oil, and 2 Tbsp. thyme. Sprinkle breadcrumb mixture over vegetables. Bake, uncovered, 30 more minutes or until breadcrumbs are browned and liquid almost evaporates. Let stand 10 minutes before serving.

Yield: 10 servings.

Potato-Butternut Squash-and-Gruyère Gratin

prep: 35 min. • **cook:** 1 hr., 18 min.

5   medium-size Yukon gold
    potatoes (about 2½ lb.)
1   large butternut squash
    (about 2 lb.)
2   Tbsp. butter
1   large sweet onion, chopped
1   tsp. salt
½   tsp. pepper
2   cups (8 oz.) shredded Gruyère
    cheese
Cream Sauce

1. Preheat oven to 350°. Peel and thinly slice potatoes. Peel, seed, and thinly slice squash.
2. Cook potatoes in boiling water to cover in a Dutch oven 5 minutes. Add squash; cover and cook 3 more minutes. Remove from heat; drain well.
3. Melt butter in a large skillet over medium heat; add onion, and sauté 10 to 12 minutes or until golden brown.
4. Layer half of potato slices and squash in a lightly greased 13- x 9-inch baking dish; sprinkle with half of salt and pepper. Top with half of onion, cheese, and Cream Sauce. Repeat layers, ending with Cream Sauce.
5. Bake at 350° for 1 hour or until golden brown. **Yield:** 10 to 12 servings.

Use a serrated peeler to peel the squash, cut the squash in half lengthwise, and scoop away the seeds with a spoon.

cream sauce

prep: 5 min. • **cook:** 9 min.

¼   cup butter
⅓   cup all-purpose flour
2½ cups milk
1   cup dry white wine
¼   tsp. salt

1. Melt butter in a heavy saucepan over low heat; whisk in flour until smooth. Cook, whisking constantly, 1 minute. Gradually whisk in milk and wine; cook over medium heat, whisking constantly, 8 to 10 minutes or until mixture is thickened and bubbly. Stir in salt. **Yield:** 3½ cups.

Sweet Potato Galette

prep: 15 min. · **cook:** 30 min.

Enjoy sweet potatoes in this tart-like presentation. Freshly grated nutmeg adds a spicy, sweet flavor.

2   lb. sweet potatoes, peeled and sliced into ⅛-inch-thick rounds

¼   cup unsalted butter, melted and divided

2   Tbsp. all-purpose flour

1   tsp. salt

½   tsp. pepper

¼   tsp. freshly grated nutmeg

1. Preheat oven to 375°. Combine sweet potatoes and 2 Tbsp. butter in a large bowl, tossing to coat. Combine flour and next 3 ingredients; sprinkle over potatoes. Toss potatoes to coat.

2. Place 2 Tbsp. butter in a 10-inch cast-iron skillet or other large ovenproof skillet. Arrange 1 layer of sweet potatoes in slightly overlapping concentric circles in skillet. Top with remaining sweet potatoes.

3. Cut a circle of nonstick aluminum foil; place over potatoes. Place a 9-inch cast-iron skillet on top of foil to weight the galette. Cook galette over medium heat 5 minutes without disturbing. Transfer weighted skillet to oven; bake at 375° for 10 minutes. Remove top skillet and foil, and bake galette 15 more minutes or until potatoes are tender. Loosen edges of galette with a spatula to prevent sticking. Invert onto serving plate; serve warm. **Yield:** 6 servings.

Skillet Grits With Seasoned Vegetables

prep: 10 min. • cook: 18 min.

1 (32-oz.) container chicken broth
3 Tbsp. butter
1 tsp. salt
1½ cups uncooked regular grits
1 cup (4 oz.) shredded Cheddar cheese
⅓ cup (1.5 oz.) shredded Parmesan cheese
½ tsp. pepper
Seasoned Vegetables

1. Bring first 3 ingredients to a boil in a large sauce-pan over medium-high heat. Gradually whisk in grits, return to a boil. Reduce heat to medium-low, and simmer, stirring occasionally, 10 to 12 minutes or until thickened.

2. Whisk in cheeses and pepper until cheeses are melted. Spoon Seasoned Vegetables evenly over grits, and serve immediately. **Yield:** 6 to 8 servings.

This is a robust, meatless recipe that you can prep in advance. Start by cooking the vegetables. If you make the vegetables a day ahead, cook them a few minutes less to ensure they don't overcook when they're reheated.

seasoned vegetables

prep: 20 min. • cook: 25 min.

1 medium onion, chopped
2 garlic cloves, minced
2 Tbsp. olive oil
4 carrots, chopped
3 small red potatoes, diced
2 small turnips (about ½ lb.), peeled and chopped
2 celery ribs, diced
1 medium zucchini, chopped
1 (14-oz.) can chicken broth
1 tsp. salt
1 tsp. dried thyme
½ tsp. pepper
1 tsp. cornstarch
1 Tbsp. water

1. Sauté onion and garlic in hot oil in a large skillet over medium heat 5 minutes or until caramelized. Add carrots and next 4 ingredients, and sauté 12 to 15 minutes or until vegetables are tender. Increase heat to medium-high; stir in chicken broth and next 3 ingredients. Bring to a boil. Reduce heat to medium-low, and simmer, stirring occasionally, 5 minutes.

2. Whisk together cornstarch and 1 Tbsp. water until smooth. Whisk into vegetable mixture in skillet, and cook, stirring constantly, 3 to 5 minutes or until thickened. **Yield:** 6 to 8 servings.

Citrus Salad With Orange Vinaigrette

prep: 30 min. • **cook: 6 min.**

2 Tbsp. chopped walnuts or pecans (optional)
1 (5-oz.) bag mixed baby greens, thoroughly washed
2 navel oranges, peeled and sectioned
1 large grapefruit, peeled and sectioned
1 pear, peeled and thinly sliced
1 cup seedless red grapes
Orange Vinaigrette

1. Preheat oven to 350°. Bake nuts in a single layer in a shallow pan 6 to 8 minutes or until toasted and fragrant

2. Place greens in a large bowl. Add orange sections, grapefruit sections, sliced pear, and grapes. Drizzle with ¼ cup Orange Vinaigrette, tossing gently to coat. Sprinkle toasted nuts over salad, and serve immediately with remaining vinaigrette. **Yield:** 6 servings.

To speed up the prep time for this salad, you can skip the nuts. It's delicious either way.

orange vinaigrette

prep: 10 min.

¼ cup white wine vinegar
2 tsp. orange zest
3 Tbsp. fresh orange juice
1 Tbsp. sugar
½ tsp. salt
½ tsp. pepper
¾ cup olive oil

1. Whisk together first 6 ingredients in a small bowl; add oil in a slow steady stream, whisking until blended. **Yield:** about 1¼ cups.

tips from our kitchen

Orange Know-how When using oranges in recipes, here's a quick guide: 2 to 4 medium oranges will yield about 1 cup juice, and it takes 2 medium oranges to yield a cup of bite-size pieces. Each orange usually contains 10 to 12 sections, and will produce around 4 tsp. of zest.

Fruit Salad With Lemon-Mint Syrup

prep: 27 min. • **cook: 2 min.**

You can prepare the syrup up to 1 day ahead, and refrigerate it until ready to assemble the salad.

1 (24-oz.) jar sliced mangos in light syrup
1 large lemon
5 fresh mint leaves, crushed
4 large kiwifruit, peeled, halved lengthwise, and sliced
3 cups seedless red grapes
1 cup seedless green grapes
1 pomegranate, seeds removed and reserved
Garnish: fresh mint

1. Drain mangos, reserving 1 cup syrup. Peel 3 strips of lemon rind with a vegetable peeler; juice lemon to measure 3 Tbsp. Combine reserved syrup, lemon rind, lemon juice, and crushed mint leaves in a small microwave-safe bowl. Cover and microwave at HIGH 2 minutes or until syrup begins to bubble. Cover and cool completely; chill.
2. Cut mango slices into cubes, and place in a large bowl; add kiwifruit, grapes, and pomegranate seeds. Remove lemon rind and mint from syrup with a slotted spoon. Pour syrup over fruit; toss. Cover and chill until ready to serve. Garnish, if desired. **Yield:** 16 servings.

Grapefruit Compote in Rosemary Syrup

prep: 20 min. • **cook: 5 min.**

Serve this in shallow bowls and include a little syrup with each serving—the rosemary-flavored syrup is the best part! If a little of the syrup remains at the end, section another grapefruit into the syrup, and chill it for another day.

1 cup sugar
½ cup water
3 Tbsp. honey
3 sprigs fresh rosemary
6 large grapefruit
½ cup maraschino cherries with stems
Garnish: fresh rosemary sprigs

1. Combine first 4 ingredients in a saucepan; bring to a boil over medium heat. Boil 5 minutes. Remove from heat, and let cool completely. Remove and discard rosemary.
2. Section grapefruit over a large bowl, catching juices. Pour rosemary syrup over fruit in bowl. Add cherries. Cover and chill until ready to serve or up to 3 days. Garnish, if desired. **Yield:** 8 to 10 servings.

Fruit Salad With
Lemon-Mint Syrup

Warm Bean Salad With Olives

prep: 23 min. • **cook: 9 min.**

This Tuscan-inspired salad partners well with a roasted chicken entrée.

2 cups small cauliflower florets
½ cup extra virgin olive oil, divided
1 cup diced celery
1 cup diced red onion
2 garlic cloves, minced
⅓ cup white wine vinegar
1 Tbsp. honey
2 (15.5-oz.) cans cannellini beans, rinsed and drained
1 (7-oz.) jar pitted kalamata olives, halved
2 Tbsp. chopped fresh parsley
1 Tbsp. chopped fresh sage
1 tsp. salt
¼ tsp. freshly ground pepper
Garnish: fresh sage

1. Cook cauliflower in boiling water to cover 5 to 6 minutes or until crisp-tender. Plunge into ice water to stop the cooking process; drain and set aside.

2. Heat ¼ cup olive oil in a large skillet over medium-high heat until hot. Add celery and onion; sauté 3 minutes or until almost tender. Add garlic; sauté 30 seconds. Stir in vinegar and honey, stirring to dissolve honey.

3. Combine cauliflower and sautéed vegetables in a large bowl. Add remaining ¼ cup olive oil, beans, and next 5 ingredients; stir well to combine. Serve warm or at room temperature. Garnish, if desired. **Yield:** 6 to 8 servings.

Cabbage and Apple Salad With Roasted Onions

prep: 37 min.   •   cook: 31 min.

2   (10-oz.) packages fresh pearl
     onions
1   head red cabbage, shredded
2   Tbsp. salt
2   Tbsp. olive oil
6   Tbsp. white wine vinegar,
     divided
6   Tbsp. maple syrup, divided
2   cups chopped pecans, toasted
     and divided
1   cup sour cream
½   tsp. salt
4   Granny Smith apples,
     chopped
1   head curly endive, chopped

1. Preheat oven to 450°. Trim bottom ends of onions. Blanch unpeeled onions, in batches, in rapidly boiling water in a large saucepan 45 seconds. (It's important to blanch in batches so that the water remains at a boil.) Drain and peel onions; place in a large zip-top freezer bag, seal, and refrigerate overnight, if desired.

2. Combine cabbage and 2 Tbsp. salt in a large bowl; let stand 30 minutes, tossing occasionally. Rinse thoroughly, and drain well.

3. Combine onions and oil in a shallow roasting pan or a large cast-iron skillet; toss to coat. Spread onions in a single layer. Roast at 450° for 25 minutes or until browned, stirring after 20 minutes.

4. Combine ¼ cup each vinegar and maple syrup; add to roasted onions. Roast 5 more minutes or until slightly thickened and onions are glazed. Set aside.

5. Combine remaining 2 Tbsp. vinegar, 2 Tbsp. maple syrup, 1 cup chopped pecans, sour cream, and ½ tsp. salt in a food processor or blender; process 1 to 2 minutes or until smooth. Cover and chill dressing overnight, if desired.

6. Toss together chopped apple, cabbage, and endive in a large bowl. Drizzle each serving with dressing, and top with roasted onions; sprinkle with remaining 1 cup pecans. **Yield:** 8 servings.

note: For convenience, blanch and peel pearl onions a day ahead; store in refrigerator. Prepare dressing up to a day ahead, and store in refrigerator.

It's worth the time to blanch and peel pearl onions for this salad. We don't recommend using frozen pearl onions. Use a large slotted spoon to corral the onions and keep the process simple.

Cranberry-Apple-Filled Walnut Cake Roll

prep: 18 min. • cook: 22 min.

2   large cooking apples, peeled, cored, and chopped
1   cup fresh cranberries
¼   cup sugar
¼   cup water
2   Tbsp. brandy
1   tsp. lemon juice
½   tsp. ground cinnamon
¼   tsp. ground nutmeg
⅔   cup all-purpose flour
1   tsp. baking powder
¼   tsp. salt
3   large eggs
¾   cup sugar
⅓   cup water
1   tsp. vanilla extract
⅓   cup ground walnuts
2   to 3 Tbsp. powdered sugar
1   cup whipping cream
½   tsp. ground cinnamon
1   tsp. vanilla extract
Garnish: coarsely chopped walnuts

1. Preheat oven to 375°. Coat a 15- x 10- x 1-inch jelly roll pan with cooking spray. Line bottom of pan with wax paper; coat wax paper with cooking spray. Set aside.

2. Combine first 8 ingredients in a medium saucepan. Cook over medium heat about 10 minutes or until cranberry skins pop and liquid is absorbed, stirring occasionally. Let cool completely.

3. Combine flour, baking powder, and salt; set aside. Beat eggs in a large mixing bowl at high speed of an electric mixer 2 minutes. Gradually add ¾ cup sugar, beating 5 minutes or until thick and pale. Stir in ⅓ cup water and 1 tsp. vanilla. Gradually fold flour mixture and ground walnuts into egg mixture with a wire whisk. Spread batter evenly in prepared pan.

4. Bake at 375° for 12 minutes or until cake springs back when lightly touched in the center.

5. Sift powdered sugar in a 15- x 10-inch rectangle on a cloth towel. When cake is done, immediately loosen from sides of pan, and turn out onto towel. Peel off wax paper. Starting at narrow end, roll up cake and towel together; place, seam side down, on a wire rack to cool.

6. Unroll cake; spread with cranberry mixture. Reroll cake without towel; place, seam side down, on a serving plate.

7. Beat whipping cream, ½ tsp. ground cinnamon, and 1 tsp. vanilla at high speed until stiff peaks form. Spread mixture over cake, or, if desired, pipe it over cake. To pipe it, spoon mixture into a decorating bag fitted with a large flower tip (we used Wilton No. 1E), and pipe icing in strips to cover cake. Garnish, if desired. **Yield:** 6 servings.

This cake roll is filled with all the best ingredients of the season—apples, cranberries, and walnuts—with sprinklings of cinnamon and nutmeg.

Clementine-Gingersnap Trifles

prep: 30 min. • **other: 2 hr.**

Clementines, a variety of Mandarin orange, are plentiful in winter. In a pinch, substitute 2 (29-oz.) cans mandarin oranges in light syrup, drained.

1 (8-oz.) package cream cheese, softened
¼ cup sugar
1 tsp. lemon zest
1 tsp. vanilla extract, divided
¾ cup heavy cream, whipped
10 to 12 clementines
¼ cup orange marmalade
1½ tsp. poppy seeds
1 (5.25-oz.) package thin ginger cookies
Garnishes: sliced kiwi, thin ginger cookies

1. Beat cream cheese, sugar, zest, and ½ tsp. vanilla at medium-high speed with a heavy-duty electric stand mixer 30 seconds or until smooth and sugar is dissolved. Fold in whipped cream, and spoon into a 1-gal. zip-top plastic bag. Seal bag, and chill 2 to 24 hours.

2. Peel clementines, and separate into segments. (Yield should be 4 cups.)

3. Microwave marmalade in a medium bowl at HIGH 20 seconds or until melted. Stir in clementine segments, poppy seeds, and remaining ½ tsp. vanilla. Remove and reserve 6 segments. Divide half of clementine mixture among 6 (10- to 13-oz.) glasses. Top each with 2 cookies. Repeat layers once.

4. Snip 1 corner of bag with cream cheese mixture with scissors to make a 1-inch hole. Pipe mixture onto cookies in glasses. Serve immediately, or cover and chill 2 hours. Top with reserved segments just before serving, and garnish, if desired. **Yield:** 6 servings.

note: For testing purposes only, we used Anna's Ginger Thins. A 2½- to 3-qt. trifle dish may be substituted for 6 (10- to 13-oz.) glasses.

Lightened Clementine-Gingersnap Trifles: Substitute reduced-fat cream cheese for regular cream cheese and 1 (8-oz.) container reduced-fat whipped topping, thawed, for whipped heavy cream. Decrease sugar to 1 Tbsp. Proceed with recipe as directed.

Sautéed Brown Sugar Pears

prep: 15 min. · **cook: 5 min.**

1   Tbsp. lemon juice
3   Anjou pears, peeled and
    quartered
3   Tbsp. butter, divided
¼   cup firmly packed brown
    sugar
1   tsp. vanilla extract
Crème fraîche or vanilla ice
    cream
Gingersnaps, crumbled

1. Sprinkle lemon juice over pears; toss. Melt 1 Tbsp. butter in a large nonstick skillet over medium-high heat. Sauté pears 2 minutes or until browned. Add remaining 2 Tbsp. butter and brown sugar to skillet. Reduce heat to medium-low; cook, stirring often, 3 to 4 minutes or until pears are tender. Remove from heat, and stir in vanilla extract. Serve warm pears and syrup with a dollop of crème fraîche or ice cream. Sprinkle with gingersnap crumbs. **Yield:** 4 servings.

A simple skillet pear dish gets dressed up with crème fraîche and gingersnap crumbs. This recipe can be doubled easily.

tips from the farm

Using Anjou Pears Egg-shaped with greenish-yellow or red skin, Anjou pears are good for slicing into salads, cooking in desserts, or baking whole, and are available from October to May.

Pecan Biscotti

prep: 23 min. • **cook: 39 min.** • **other: 10 min.**

Cornmeal adds a pleasant twist to these super crunchy cookies. Store biscotti in an airtight container to keep them fresh and crispy.

1¾ cups all-purpose flour
½ cup yellow cornmeal
1¼ tsp. baking powder
¼ tsp. salt
1 cup finely chopped pecans, toasted
2 large eggs, lightly beaten
¾ cup sugar
½ cup vegetable oil
¼ tsp. almond extract or vanilla extract

1. Preheat oven to 350°. Combine first 5 ingredients in a large bowl.

2. Stir together eggs and remaining 3 ingredients; gradually add to flour mixture, stirring just until dry ingredients are moistened.

3. Divide dough in half. With lightly floured hands, shape each portion into a 12- x 2-inch log. Place logs 3 inches apart on a lightly greased baking sheet.

4. Bake at 350° for 25 minutes. Cool logs on baking sheet 10 minutes.

5. Cut each log diagonally into ¾-inch-thick slices with a serrated knife, using a gentle sawing motion. Return slices, cut side down, to baking sheet.

6. Bake at 350° for 7 minutes. Turn biscotti over, and bake 7 more minutes. Remove to wire racks to cool completely. **Yield:** 2½ dozen.

tips from our kitchen

Biscotti Basics Biscotti are twice-baked Italian-style cookies made by baking dough as a loaf, and then slicing the loaf and baking the slices. The cookies are very crunchy, which makes them perfect for dipping into coffee.

Black-and-White
Caramel Apples

Caramel Apples

prep: 20 min. • **other: 35 min.**

6   large Granny Smith apples
6   wooden craft sticks
1   (14-oz.) bag caramels
1   Tbsp. vanilla extract
2   cups chopped pecans,
    toasted
1   (12-oz.) bag semisweet
    chocolate morsels
Pecan halves (optional)

1. Wash and dry apples; remove stems. Insert craft sticks into stem end of each apple; set aside.
2. Combine caramels, vanilla, and 1 Tbsp. water in a microwave-safe glass bowl. Microwave on HIGH 90 seconds or until melted, stirring twice.
3. Quickly dip each apple into the caramel mixture, allowing excess caramel to drip off. Roll in chopped pecans; place on lightly greased wax paper. Chill at least 15 minutes.
4. Microwave chocolate morsels at HIGH 90 seconds or until melted, stirring twice; cool 5 minutes. Pour chocolate where craft sticks and apple meet, allowing chocolate to drip down sides of apples. Press pecan halves onto chocolate, if desired. Chill 15 minutes or until set. **Yield:** 6 apples.

note: For testing purposes only, we used Kraft Caramels.

Black-and-White Caramel Apples: Microwave 6 oz. white chocolate morsels at HIGH 60 seconds or until melted, stirring once; drizzle evenly over semisweet chocolate.

Place these tasty treats in cellophane bags for easy gift-giving.

fresh produce & herb primer

Selecting and properly storing fresh produce and herbs are key factors in getting the best flavor from just-picked ingredients. This primer provides tips on selecting, storing, preparing, and cooking a variety of fruits, vegetables, and herbs.

spring

bananas
select: Choose ripe bananas for immediate use and ones that are still slightly green for later use. Bananas should be without bruises, full and plump, and bright in color.
store: Store bananas at room temperature until ripe; then refrigerate. The peel will turn black once refrigerated, but the meat will remain firm and white for several days.
prepare: Bananas are usually eaten fresh, requiring no preparation.
cook: Dry, bake, fry, boil, steam, and sauté to add sweet flavor to both savory and sweet dishes.

pineapples
select: A fresh pineapple should have firm green leaves on its top, and the body should be firm.
store: Pineapple will not become sweeter once picked, but will soften if left at room temperature for a few days. It should be refrigerated and used as soon as possible. Cut pineapple will last a few more days if placed in a tightly covered container and refrigerated or frozen.
prepare: To peel a pineapple, slice off the bottom and the green top. Stand the pineapple on one cut end, and slice off the skin, cutting just below the surface in wide vertical strips, leaving the small brown eyes. Remove the eyes by cutting diagonally around the fruit, following the pattern of the eyes and making shallow, narrow furrows, cutting away as little of the flesh as possible. Slice the pineapple into rings, and use a round cookie cutter or knife to remove the core.
cook: Pineapple is used in desserts, salads, and as a marinade and garnish for meats and seafood.

strawberries
select: Choose brightly colored berries that still have their green caps attached.
store: Store in a moisture-proof container in the refrigerator for 3 to 4 days.
prepare: Do not wash or remove the hulls until you're ready to use the strawberries.
cook: It's best not to overwhelm the fresh flavor of strawberries. Try a mousse or a simple, sweet soup—or toss the berries with fresh salad greens.

Valencia oranges
select: Choose firm Valencias that have smooth skins. Don't worry about brown patches on the skin; this does not indicate poor quality.
store: Store Valencias at room temperature up to 1 week or refrigerate up to 3 weeks.
prepare: Peel Valencias with a paring knife. Hold it over a bowl to catch the juices, slice between the membranes and one side of one segment, and lift the segment out.
To cook: For the best flavor, use Valencias raw. If they are cooked, cook them only briefly.

artichokes
select: Look for heavy, compact artichokes that have deep green, tight leaves.
store: Store artichokes in a plastic bag in the refrigerator up to 1 week.
prepare: Hold artichokes by the stem, and plunge them up and down in cold water. Cut off stems, and trim about ½ inch from the top. Remove any loose bottom leaves, and trim approximately ¼ off the top of each outer leaf.
cook: Artichokes can be grilled, steamed, roasted, fried, or sautéed. When cooking, use stainless steel cookware and add a little lemon juice to the water to keep the leaves from darkening.

arugula

select: Leaves should be bright green and crisp; stems shouldn't be withered or slimy.
store: Wrap a moist paper towel around the bunch, and store it up to 2 days. Dirt particles cling tightly to the leaves, so wash them well, and spin them dry just before using.
prepare: Make sure to remove any wilted leaves.
cook: Arugula is most commonly used as a salad green. It can also be wilted like spinach.

asparagus

select: Look for asparagus with smooth skin, uniform color, and a dry, compact tip.
store: It's okay to wrap them in damp paper towels for several days; to extend their life, refrigerate stalks, tips up, in a cup of shallow water. Don't freeze fresh asparagus.
prepare: Snap fibrous ends from asparagus spears. Cook asparagus as is, or peel the skin with a vegetable peeler to make the stalks more tender.
cook: Broil, steam, grill, roast, or sautée for a few minutes until crisp-tender.

baby leeks

select: Choose leeks with clean, white bulbs and firm, tightly-rolled dark green tops.
store: Refrigerate leeks in a plastic bag up to 5 days.
prepare: Because leeks grow partly underground, they are often very dirty. To clean, trim off the roots and the tough tops of the green leaves. Then cut the leek stalk in half, and rinse well.
cook: Leeks can be cooked whole or chopped and sliced for salads, soups, or other dishes.

dandelion greens

select: The most tender dandelion greens are found in early spring.
store: Refrigerate dandelion greens in a plastic bag up to 5 days.
prepare: Wash the leaves thoroughly before using.
cook: The leaves can be cooked like spinach; the roots can be eaten as vegetables or roasted and ground to make a coffee-like beverage.

fava beans

select: Look for long, plump, heavy pods that are bright green and unblemished.
store: Keep the pods in a bag in the refrigerator up to a week; store peeled beans 1 to 2 days. You can freeze blanched, peeled beans for a couple of months.
prepare: Open the pods and remove the beans. Boil briefly, then remove the tough outer skin.
cook: Once blanched and peeled, they add crunch to any dish. If you prefer a softer texture, sauté or cook the blanched beans in boiling water until tender.

green onions

select: Look for healthy dark green tops on the onions. Dry, wilted, or slimy tops are signs of age.
store: Wrap green onions in plastic and refrigerate up to 3 weeks, depending on the variety.
prepare: Cut off root ends and any limp or damaged parts of the green tops. Remove the outer layers of skin before you slice or chop.
cook: Green onions can be eaten raw, sautéed, baked, blanched, grilled, or used as a garnish.

green peas

select: Look for crisp, medium-sized bright green pods; avoid full, oversized pods, which tend to hold starchy paste.
store: Shell and chill green peas as soon as possible. If you can't cook and eat fresh peas within 2 or 3 days, blanch and freeze them up to 2 months.
prepare: Green peas will open like a zipper when pressure is applied to the middle of the pod.
cook: Boil, steam, or braise peas just until tender.

lettuce

select: Look for lettuce that's unbruised, unwilted, and has robust color.

store: Refrigerate clean lettuce in a plastic bag or an airtight container up to 5 days.

prepare: Since leaves can be dirty as well as delicate, wash them gently in cool water, and then dry thoroughly. A salad spinner can be used to dry greens, or you can shake them free of excess moisture and blot dry with paper towels. Dressings cling better to dry leaves.

rhubarb

select: Choose firm, crisp, medium-sized stalks.

store: Rhubarb is highly perishable, so it should be refrigerated in a plastic bag up to 3 days. It can also be blanched and frozen in freezer containers up to 6 months.

prepare: Wash and trim the stems; remove and discard all leaves, as they are poisonous.

cook: Rhubarb is usually cooked with a generous amount of sugar to balance its tartness. It makes delicious sauces, jams, and desserts.

snap beans

select: Look for small, tender, crisp pod beans with bright color. If they're fresh, you'll hear the snap when you bend pod beans.

store: Wash fresh beans before storing them in the refrigerator in plastic bags up to 3 or 4 days.

prepare: Before you cook snap beans, wash them thoroughly, and cut off the tips.

cook: When steamed, sautéed, or simmered, this vegetable makes a popular side dish.

snow peas

select: Once picked, the sugar in snow peas quickly converts to starch, so cook them soon. You can refrigerate them in a plastic bag for a day or so before they begin to lose flavor.

store: Keep the pods in a bag in the refrigerator up to a week; store peeled beans only a day or 2. You can freeze blanched, peeled beans for a couple of months.

prepare: Snow peas are sweet and tender enough to be eaten raw or cooked whole, although it's best to pinch off the tip ends and remove any strings just before using.

cook: Snow peas are easy to cook. Drop them into boiling water and cook about 30 seconds or steam over boiling water less than a minute. They can also be stir-fried by themselves or tossed into a stir-fried recipe; add them at the last minute, and cook just until they turn bright green.

spinach

select: Select spinach bunches with crisp leaves; avoid limp bunches with yellowing leaves. Spinach is available year-round, but its peak local season is May to August.

store: If unwashed, wash in cold water, and pat dry. Chill the leaves in a plastic bag lined with damp paper towels up to 3 days.

prepare: Spinach is usually very gritty, so make sure that it's thoroughly washed.

cook: Spinach leaves can be served cooked, as in spanakopita, or served raw in salads.

sugar snap peas

select: Choose sugar snap peas that are firm, plump, and bright green with no yellowing in color. Sugar snaps are available during spring and fall months.

store: Keep sugar snaps refrigerated in a plastic bag up to 3 or 4 days.

prepare: Sugar snaps do not require shelling or stringing. You can remove the cap end, if desired.

cook: Sugar snap peas can be served raw or briefly cooked. Whether you serve them warm or chilled, they are best blanched first.

sweet onions

select: Look for sweet onions that are light golden brown in color with a shiny tissue-thin skin and firm, tight, dry necks.

store: To extend the life of sweet onions, store them so that they aren't touching each other; some cooks hang them in old pantyhose with knots tied between each onion.

prepare: Cut through the stem end, peel back the papery skin, and cut the onion down the middle lengthwise. Place each half, cut side down, on a cutting board, make several parallel horizontal cuts almost to the root end. Then make several parallel vertical cuts through the onion layers, but again, not cutting through the root end. Finally, cut across the grain to make chopped pieces.

cook: Sweet onions can be grilled, sautéed, caramelized, baked, cooked, broiled, or eaten raw.

garlic chives

select: Fresh garlic chives should have dark green leaves and no signs of wilting.

store: Store fresh garlic chives in a plastic bag in the refrigerator up to a week.

prepare: Fresh garlic chives can be snipped with kitchen shears to the desired length.

cook: Garlic chives are often found in Chinese recipes for soups, stews, salads and marinades.

lemon grass

select: Lemon grass can be purchased fresh or dried in Asian markets and in the gourmet produce section of many supermarkets. Look for fragrant stalks that are tightly formed with a lemony green color near the bulb and a truer green color at the end of the stalk.

store: Store fresh lemon grass in the refrigerator in a tightly sealed plastic bag up to 3 weeks. You can also freeze it for about 6 months without any flavor loss.

prepare: Peel away the outer layers of leaves until you see the softer, fleshier part of the lemon grass stalk. This is what you want to use cooking.

cook: Use lemon grass in dishes such as soups and curries.

summer

blackberries

select: Select plump, well-colored berries with hulls detached. If hulls are still intact, the berries were picked too early.

store: Fresh blackberries are best stored in the refrigerator for up to a week. Choose a wide, shallow bowl to store berries, and cover with plastic wrap to keep them from drying out.

prepare: Just before you use your blackberries, rinse them under cold water. For the best flavor, allow the berries to come to room temperature.

cook: Blackberries can be eaten out of hand, in desserts, or topped with sweetened whipped cream. When pureeing blackberries, press them through a sieve to remove the seeds and pulp.

blueberries

select: Pick plump, juicy berries with blooms that have no trace of mold or discoloration. Look for firm, uniformly sized berries with deep color and no hulls or stems.

store: If eating blueberries within 24 hours of picking, store them at room temperature; otherwise, keep them refrigerated in a moisture-proof container up to 3 days.

prepare: Wash berries just before using them.

cook: Blueberries can be eaten out of hand, in pies, pancakes, salads, jams, and jellies.

cantaloupes

select: Pick a cantaloupe with a soft stem end. Look for a light yellow ridged or smooth outer shell. Avoid cantaloupe with a green cast.

store: Store unripe cantaloupes at room temperature and ripe cantaloupes in the refrigerator for 1 to 2 days.

prepare: Wash cantaloupe in warm soapy water before cutting to get rid of any impurity on the rind that might be carried from the knife blade to the flesh. Remove all seeds and strings.

cook: Cantaloupe can be served many ways, including chutneys, salads, and beverages.

cherries

select: Choose cherries with firm, smooth, unblemished skins with stems still attached.

store: Fresh cherries should be eaten as soon as possible; they can be covered and refrigerated up to 4 days. After opening canned cherries, store them in an airtight container in the refrigerator up to a week. Maraschino cherries last up to 6 months in the refrigerator.

prepare: The quickest way to pit fresh cherries is with a cherry pitter. If you don't have one, try this: push the cherry firmly down onto the pointed end of a pastry bag tip, or push a drinking straw through the bottom of the cherry, forcing the pit up and out through the stem end.

cook: Sweet cherries can be eaten out of hand; sour cherries are great in desserts and sauces.

honeydew melons

select: Fresh, ripe honeydews should have a soft, velvety texture and be heavy for their size.

store: Ripe honeydews will keep up to 5 days in the refrigerator or in a cool, dark place. Seal in plastic wrap or an airtight container; they readily absorb odors and flavors of other foods.

prepare: Wash honeydew before cutting. Cut the melon in half, and scoop out the seeds.

cook: You can serve honeydew alone, or mix it up with other fresh fruits for a summer salad. Honeydew can be pureed and made into a cold soup or used in a smoothie.

nectarines

select: Nectarines should be plump, rich in color, and have a softening along the seam.

store: Speed the nectarines ripening by placing them in a paper bag for several days at room temperature. Once ripened, store nectarines in the refrigerator, and use within 2 or 3 days.

prepare: Nectarines can be eaten out of hand or used in a variety of salads and desserts.

cook: Nectarines can be grilled or used in dishes including pork, chicken, and fish.

peaches

select: Look for peaches that are firm with a taut, unblemished skin and no signs of bruising or wrinkles. If you smell peaches when you walk up to the stand, you know they are ripe.

store: Ripen peaches at room temperature. If ripe, put them in the refrigerator; they'll keep for a few days.

prepare: Wash, peel, if desired; and slice peaches before eating, or prepare according to recipe directions.

cook: Peaches work with both sweet and savory dishes. Cook with sugar on the stove until thickened for a delicious jam. Sautée, grill, or roast them to serve with duck, chicken, or pork.

plums

select: Choose plums that have a little give when you squeeze them and a sweet-smelling aroma.

store: Firm plums can be stored at room temperature until they become slightly soft. Refrigerate ripe plums in a plastic bag up to 4 or 5 days.

prepare: Wash your plum before you eat it. Try slicing up a plum, and throw it in a salad or slaw.

cook: Plums can be used for fruit compotes, desserts, jams, jellies, sauces, snacks, and tarts.

raspberries

select: Fresh, ripe raspberries should be plump and tender, but not mushy. Raspberries are sold in clear packaging, so make sure to check all sides for signs of poor quality.

store: Store in an airtight container in the refrigerator for 2 to 3 days.

prepare: Rinse raspberries lightly under cold water just before using them.

cook: Add raspberries to pancakes or waffles, or make them into jellies and jams.

watermelons

select: Choose a firm, symmetrical, unblemished watermelon with a dull rind, without cracks or soft spots, that barely yields to pressure.

store: Store uncut at room temperature up to 1 week. Refrigerate 8 to 10 hours to serve chilled.

prepare: Wash and dry the rind before cutting to prevent bacterial contamination. Once sliced, cover with plastic wrap; refrigerate up to 4 days.

cook: Use watermelon to make glazes or sauces. It can also be grilled and stir-fried.

carrots

select: Choose carrots that are firm and brightly colored, avoiding ones that are cracked. If the leafy tops are attached, make sure they are not wilted.

store: Remove tops if attached; place carrots in plastic bags, and refrigerate up to 2 weeks.

prepare: Wash and cut carrots into sticks for dipping and eating, or shred them to add to salads or slaw.

cook: You can steam, braise, sauté, bake, or microwave your carrots. Add them to soups and stews, or serve them as a side dish.

celery

select: Choose celery that is bright in color, firm, and brittle. Avoid stalks with wilted leaves.

store: Store celery in a plastic bag in the refrigerator, leaving the ribs attached to the stalk until ready to use. It will typically keep up to a couple of weeks.

prepare: To restore crispness to fresh celery, trim ribs and soak them in ice water 15 minutes.

cook: Celery is a popular ingredient in soups and stews. It is also commonly used in stuffing recipes, stir-fries, or salad dressings. Cut into strips for dipping.

collards

select: Young collards with small leaves are more tender and less bitter. Avoid collards with large leathery leaves that are withered or that have yellow spots.

store: Wash collards, and pat dry. Place them in a plastic bag, and refrigerate up to 5 days.

prepare: Make sure you wash collard green leaves by hand, once in warm water and three times in cold water, to get rid of all the grit. Like all greens, collards cook down considerably. A good rule of thumb is that 1 pound of raw greens yields 1½ cups cooked.

cook: Collards are traditionally cooked in a pork-seasoned broth to tame bitter flavors.

corn

select: A fresh husk is the number one thing to look for. Deep brown silk tips or ends mean it's ripe, but the whole silk shouldn't be dried up. Open the tip of the husk to see if the kernels are all the way to the end of the ear; kernels should be plump and milky when pinched.

store: The sugars in corn begin to turn to starch as soon as it's harvested, so plan to eat it as soon as possible. You can store it in its husk in the refrigerator up to a day.

prepare: Sweet summer corn requires minimal preparation and cooking.

cook: Place husked ears in a pot of cold water; bring water to a boil. Once the water boils, remove from heat, and let stand 1 minute before serving. Serve it on the cob, or cut the kernels off to use in soups, salads, succotash, salsas, and other dishes.

cucumbers

select: Choose cucumbers with a deep green color. Avoid soft patches or shriveled ends.
store: Refrigerate cucumbers up to 2 weeks. Use pickling cucumbers soon after picking.
prepare: If you don't peel your cucumbers, make sure you wash the waxy finish off before using.
cook: Cucumbers are best eaten raw and are traditionally used as a basic salad ingredient or on vegetable trays. They can also be sliced, dipped in batter, and fried.

green beans

select: Look for small, tender, crisp pod beans with bright color that snap when you bend them.
store: Fresh beans should be washed before being stored in the refrigerator in plastic bags up to 3 or 4 days.
prepare: Although they are generally cooked, green beans can be eaten raw. Just rinse them and snap them into bite-sized pieces.
cook: To retain nutrients, cook green beans a minimal amount of time. They should keep their bright color when cooked. Steaming or stir-frying works best.

lima beans

select: Fresh limas are available from June to September and are usually sold in their pods.
store: Store dried beans at room temperature in tightly covered containers up to 1 year, or freeze up to 2 years.
prepare: Shell fresh limas before eating them. Dried beans require soaking before cooking.
cook: Limas can be used as a side dish, an ingredient in soups, or cooked and cooled for salads.

okra

select: Choose tender, bright green pods free of damage.
store: Store okra in a plastic bag in the refrigerator up to 3 days.
prepare: Make sure to rinse and pat dry your okra before using. Unless you want to use okra for its thickening effect, don't cut the pods; just remove the tip of the stem.
cook: Okra can be fried, steamed, or grilled.

peas

select: Fresh peas should have a good green color.
store: Store fresh peas in a plastic bag in the refrigerator.
prepare: The sugar in fresh peas quickly converts to starch, so it's important that they be prepared and eaten as soon as possible after picking, usually within 2 to 3 days.
cook: Peas do not require long cooking times because of their natural tenderness.

summer squash

select: Choose small, firm squash with bright-colored, blemish-free skins.
store: Refrigerate in plastic bags up to 5 days before cooking.
prepare: Summer squash is great for blending with other ingredients or in simple preparations highlighting the taste of fresh herbs. Delicate yellow squash is perfect in chilled soups.
cook: Because it has a high water content, summer squash doesn't require much cooking.

tomatoes

select: Smell them—a good tomato should smell like a tomato, especially at the stem end.
store: Place tomatoes at room temperature in a single layer, shoulder side up, and out of direct sunlight. To store ripe tomatoes for any extended period, keep them between 55º and 65º.
prepare: If you want to seed a tomato, core it, and then cut it in half crosswise. Use your thumbs to push the seeds out of the tomato halves. Seed tomatoes when you don't want much juice.
cook: Tomatoes can be stewed or crushed for use in casseroles, chili, and many Italian dishes.

basil

select: Look for leaves that show no signs of wilting. Colors vary from shades of green to purple.
store: Store basil in a plastic bag in the refrigerator.
prepare: Slice basil by rolling up a small bunch of leaves and snipping it into shreds with kitchen shears. To chop it, snip the shreds crosswise.
cook: Use basil in salads, pestos, pasta dishes, pizza, and meat and poultry dishes.

cilantro

select: When choosing cilantro, make sure you see no signs of wilting on the leaves.
store: Store in the refrigerator in a plastic bag up to a week.
cook: Cilantro is popular in Mexican, Asian, and Caribbean cuisines. Adding a tablespoon not only jazzes up a dish, it also offers a good bit of vitamin A.

lavender

select: When choosing fresh lavender, look for herbs that show no signs of wilting.
store: Treat fresh herbs like a bouquet of flowers. Douse the leaves with cool water, and wrap the stems in a damp paper towel. Place the towel-wrapped herbs in a zip-top plastic bag, remove as much air as possible from the bag, and refrigerate up to a week.
prepare: To chop fresh lavender, stuff the leaves into a glass measuring cup, and insert kitchen shears or scissors; snip in cup, rotating shears with each snip.
cook: Use lavender flowers and their leaves in desserts, marinades, and sauces.

lemon balm

select: When choosing fresh lemon balm, look for leaves that show no signs of wilting.
store: Douse with cool water, and wrap the stems in a damp paper towel. Place herbs in a zip-top plastic bag, remove as much air as possible from the bag, and refrigerate up to a week.
prepare: To chop fresh lemon balm, stuff the leaves into a glass measuring cup and insert kitchen shears or scissors; snip in cup, rotating shears with each snip.
cook: Chop leaves to use in tea bread, scones, and salads, or use leaves whole in cold beverages.

oregano

select: Choose fresh oregano that is vibrant green in color with firm stems. They should be free from darks spots or yellowing.
store: Keep fresh oregano in the refrigerator wrapped in a slightly damp paper towel. You can also freeze oregano, either whole or chopped, in airtight containers.
prepare: Oregano should be added toward the end of the cooking process since heat can easily cause a loss of its delicate flavor.
cook: Add to meat, fish, eggs, fresh and cooked tomatoes, vegetables, beans, and marinades.

autumn

figs

select: Don't judge by looks alone. A shrunken and wrinkled fig may actually be a better choice. Small cracks won't affect the flavor. Ripe figs should be heavy for their size.
store: Fresh figs are extremely perishable; handle them gently. Use them soon after purchasing, or store them in the refrigerator in a single layer no more than 2 or 3 days.
prepare: Fresh figs are best when simply prepared to enhance their natural sweetness.
cook: Fresh figs are most commonly used in desserts. Use figs in recipes including chutneys, sauces, and salads. They are also a flavorful companion for braised meats and poultry.

grapes

select: Look for grapes that are plump and securely attached to their stem. Avoid grapes that are withered, soft or bruised.

store: Store grapes, unwashed, in plastic bags, in the refrigerator, up to a week.

prepare: Always wash grapes thoroughly before eating.

cook: Use grapes to make delicious jellies and jams, or add to salads, yogurt, or as a garnish.

pears

select: Apply light thumb pressure near the pear's stem. If it is ripe, there will be a slight give.

store: If pears aren't quite ripe, place them on a kitchen counter in a brown paper bag. Once ripened, fresh pears will keep for several days in the refrigerator. Don't store them in plastic bags.

prepare: To core a pear, cut it in half lengthwise, and scoop out the core with a melon baller or grapefruit spoon. Toss cut pears with a little citrus or pineapple juice to prevent discoloring.

cook: Use ripe pears in desserts, pancakes, and meat dishes. The best pears for cooking are varieties such as Bosc, Comice, Seckel, and red and green Anjous.

persimmons

select: Choose persimmons that are medium to large in size and uniform in color. Avoid fruit that has cracks or signs of decay.

store: Always allow persimmons to ripen at room temperature; the Hachiya will be soft to the touch when ripe, but the Fuyu will be firm. Once ripened, refrigerate persimmons, and use as soon as possible, or place them in an airtight container whole and freeze up to 3 months.

prepare: Fuyu persimmons can be eaten raw as a snack, but make sure that they are ripe, as unripe persimmons are sour.

cook: Add persimmons to quick breads or desserts. They also make tasty jams and jellies.

bell peppers

select: Bell peppers are at their best from July through September. Look for firm, nicely colored fruit that is fragrant at the stem end. Avoid peppers that are damp, because they can mold.

store: Store peppers in a plastic bag in the refrigerator up to a week. They can also be sliced or chopped and frozen in a freezer bag up to 6 months.

prepare: Be sure to wash peppers just before using.

cook: Bell peppers can be roasted, stuffed, stir-fried, or used in casseroles and salads.

broccoli

select: Look for firm stalks with tightly bunched heads. If the heads show signs of buds beginning to turn yellow, it's over the hill.

store: Refrigerate fresh broccoli in a plastic bag up to 4 days. To revive broccoli, trim ½ inch from the base of the stalk and set the head in a glass of cold water in the refrigerator overnight.

prepare: When serving broccoli raw, trim it down into florets.

cook: Broccoli can be steamed, stir-fried, or cooked in the microwave. It is great on vegetable trays with dip or in green salads.

cabbage

select: Choose heads that are compact and heavy for their size. The outer leaves should be without defect and have good green or red color.

store: Refrigerate cabbage, wrapped in plastic wrap, up to 1 week. Don't cut or shred it until ready to use to maximize freshness, color, and nutrients.

prepare: Always wash the cabbage head before use. To shred cabbage quickly, quarter it, cut away the core, and thinly slice the quarters into shreds.

cook: Cabbage can be steamed, boiled, roasted, stir-fried, or used in casseroles, soups, and stews.

cauliflower

select: Cauliflower heads should be tightly packed. Avoid heads that have browning on them.

store: Wrap fresh cauliflower in plastic wrap, and refrigerate 3 to 5 days. Once cooked, it can be refrigerated 1 to 3 days.

prepare: Cauliflower should be washed and removed from the stem before using. Cut it into bite-sized florets, which are great for dipping or eating in salads.

cook: Cauliflower can be boiled, baked, and sautéed; the whole cauliflower head may be cooked in one piece and topped with sauce.

eggplant

select: Choose a firm, smooth-skinned eggplant, avoiding soft or brown spots.

store: Refrigerate fresh, uncut eggplant up to 2 days.

prepare: The eggplant's skin should be washed thoroughly before preparing. Because eggplant flesh discolors rapidly, cut it just before using. The cut flesh can be brushed with lemon juice or dipped in a mixture of lemon juice and water to prevent browning.

cook: Eggplants can be baked, broiled, fried, and grilled.

leeks

select: Buy leeks with crisp leaves and blemish-free stalks.

store: Keep leeks tightly wrapped in the refrigerator up to 5 days.

prepare: Cut the bulb in half lengthwise, and wash thoroughly, removing any soil or grit. Trim the root and leaf ends, discarding tough and withered leaves.

cook: Use leeks in quiches, risottos, pillars, soups, and stews. When preparing leeks, be attentive; they overcook easily. They're ready when the base can be pierced with a knife.

mushrooms

select: When buying fresh mushrooms, choose those that are smooth and have a dry top.

store: Refrigerate fresh mushrooms, unwashed, for no more than 3 days; they're best kept in a paper or cloth bag that allows them to breathe. Do not store mushrooms in plastic.

prepare: Clean fresh mushrooms with a mushroom brush or damp paper towel just before using. Never clean fresh mushrooms by soaking them in water. You can give them a quick rinse and pat them dry when you're about to use them.

cook: Sauté, microwave, roast, grill, broil, or use mushrooms for pizza toppings.

pumpkins

select: Look for pumpkins that are small, about 5 to 8 pounds, with tough skin. They are prized for their concentrated flavor and sweetness.

store: Store in the refrigerator up to 3 months, or in a cool, dry place up to 1 month. Once cut, wrap pumpkins tightly in plastic, refrigerate, and use within 3 or 4 days.

prepare: If you've ever carved a jack-o'-lantern, you know how to tackle a fresh pumpkin. Use your hand or a spoon to remove the seeds and stringy flesh.

cook: Go beyond traditional pumpkin dishes; quarter, steam, and mash the flesh, mixing it with black pepper or brown sugar to serve as a side dish. For a healthy snack, roast the seeds.

red potatoes

select: When buying potatoes, choose those that are firm and blemish-free. Avoid potatoes with soft spots or those that have a green cast to the skin.

store: Store potatoes in a cool, dry, dark, well-ventilated place up to 2 weeks. New potatoes should be used within 2 or 3 days of purchase.

prepare: Make sure you thoroughly wash raw potatoes before cooking to remove any dirt.

cook: Red potatoes are great for making potato salad or for pan roasting.

shallots

select: Choose shallots that are firm to the touch with a dry, papery, thin skin.

store: Store shallots in a cool, dry place up to a month.

prepare: Peel and slice or chop shallots before you use them in cooking.

cook: Use shallots in place of onions.

sweet potatoes

select: Look for small to medium sized tubers with few bruises and smooth skin.

store: Store sweet potatoes in a cool, dry, dark place. If the temperature is right (about 55°), you can keep them 3 to 4 weeks. Otherwise, use them within a week. Do not refrigerate.

prepare: Sweet potatoes can be cooked with the skin on or peeled before cooking.

cook: This versatile vegetable is best for mashing or tossing into soups and stews but can be boiled, baked, roasted, and sautéed.

Yukon gold potatoes

select: Choose potatoes that are firm and blemish-free without any soft spots.

store: Store potatoes in a cool, dry, dark, well-ventilated place up to 2 weeks.

prepare: To prepare raw potatoes for cooking, wash them thoroughly to remove any dirt.

cook: The Yukon can be baked, boiled, sautéed, or fried.

bay leaves

select: You can use fresh or dry bay leaves in your dishes. Fresh bay leaves are less available.

store: Store dry bay leaves in an airtight container in a cool, dark place up to a year.

cook: Use fresh or dried bay leaves in soups and stews. Discard whole leaves before serving food.

rosemary

select: Buy rosemary dried or fresh at your local market. You could also buy a rosemary plant and keep it in your kitchen.

store: Keep your fresh rosemary in plastic bags in the refrigerator. Store dry rosemary twigs in an airtight container, or freeze your rosemary in a freezer bag.

prepare: To harvest rosemary (from your home plant), strip the leaves from the stem.

cook: Use the strong-flavored leaves sparingly. Rosemary adds a wonderful accent to soups, meats, stews, breads, and vegetables.

sage

select: Sage is available either fresh or in three dried forms: ground, coarsely crumbled, or rubbed (finely chopped).

store: Wrap your fresh sage leaves in paper towels, and store them in a plastic bag in the refrigerator. Use within 4 to 5 days. Freeze fresh sage leaves in a freezer bag for up to a year.

cook: Sage is best known for use in holiday dressings. It also flavors sausage well, too. Sage leaves are soft and pliable, which makes them easy to tuck under poultry skin before roasting.

tarragon

select: In general, herbs should be fresh looking, crisp, and brightly colored.

store: Keep tarragon in a plastic bag with damp paper towels, and refrigerate for 1 to 2 days.

prepare: Tarragon's leaves bruise easily, so be gentle when chopping them.

cook: This leafy herb plays a classic role in Béarnaise sauce. It also adds flavor to soups, poultry, seafood, vegetables, and egg dishes. It's often used to make herb butter or vinegar.

winter

grapefruit
select: The heavier the grapefruit, the juicier it will be.
store: Grapefruits have a long shelf life and can be kept in the refrigerator for 6 to 8 weeks.
prepare: Grapefruit is most often eaten raw. It can be peeled and sectioned like oranges and added to fruit salad. Or for breakfast, cut a grapefruit in half, and eat it with a spoon.

kumquats
select: Look for kumquats with bright orange skin. Avoid any citrus with signs of decay.
store: Keep kumquats sitting out up to 1 week or refrigerated in a plastic bag for 3 to 4 weeks.
prepare: Kumquats can be sliced and served in salads or used as a garnish.
cook: Try candying or pickling whole kumquats for a delicious treat, or use them to make preserves or marmalades.

navel oranges
select: Choose from navel oranges that have smooth skins and are not moldy. Don't worry about brown patches on the skin; this does not indicate poor quality.
store: Store navel oranges at room temperature up to a week or refrigerate up to 3 weeks.
prepare: To section an orange, peel it with a paring knife. Be sure to remove the bitter white pith. Hold the orange over a bowl to catch the juices, slice between the membranes and one side of one segment of the orange. Lift the segment out with the knife blade.
use: For the best flavor, use navel oranges raw. If they are cooked, cook them only briefly.

beets
select: Look for small to medium well-shaped beets with smooth skins. Very large beets may be tough. If leaves are attached, they should be crisp and bright green.
store: A beet's leafy green tops leach nutrients from the root, so immediately trim them to about an inch. Because the greens are highly perishable, you should use them within a day. Store beets in plastic bags in the refrigerator up to 2 weeks; gently wash before use.
prepare: Because the juice can stain your hands and countertops, wear disposable latex gloves.
cook: Beets hold up well when julienned raw, roasted, baked, or broiled and pair well with orange juice, vinegar, and wine. They are often used in salads, pickles, and the soup known as borscht.

fennel
select: Look for small, heavy white fennel bulbs that are firm and free of cracks, browning, or moist areas. The stalks should be crisp with feathery, bright green fronds.
store: Store fresh fennel in a plastic bag in the refrigerator up to 5 days. Fennel seeds should be stored in a cool, dark place up to 6 months.
prepare: Before using fennel, trim the stalks about an inch above the bulb.
cook: Fennel is often added to soups and stews, and its licorice flavor becomes milder when cooked. Fennel is a good complement to seafood and poultry recipes.

parsnips
select: Because parsnips are a root vegetable, some dirt may still be on the vegetable; they should be mostly clean. Look for firm, medium-sized vegetables with uniform beige skin.
store: Keep parsnips refrigerated in a plastic bag up to a month.
prepare: Wash your parsnips before cooking. You can peel them as you would a carrot.
cook: Parsnips are suitable for baking, boiling, sautéing, roasting, or steaming and are often boiled and mashed like potatoes. They are also wonderful roasted; it brings out their sweetness.

Rutabagas

select: Rutabagas should be heavy for their size; lightweight ones tend to have a woody flavor.

store: Store rutabagas in a plastic bag in the refrigerator up to a month.

prepare: Rutabagas are coated with clear paraffin wax to hold in moisture, so make sure you wash and peel them before cooking.

cook: Rutabagas are delicious peeled and cooked as a turnip, in a small amount of water, sometimes with a little added sugar, salt, or herbs.

turnips

select: If you prefer a sweeter tasting turnip, look for small- to medium-sized vegetables.

store: Turnip roots can be refrigerated in a plastic bag for 1 to 2 weeks. Wash greens in cold water, and pat dry; store in a plastic bag lined with moist paper towels in the refrigerator up to 3 days.

prepare: Before cooking with them, wash and peel your turnip roots.

cook: Turnip roots can be boiled and mashed, or roasted and pureed, cubed and tossed with butter, or used raw in salads. Turnip greens can be boiled, steamed, sautéed, and stir-fried.

winter squash

select: The tastiest winter squash are solid and heavy with stems that are full, firm, and have a corky feel. The skin of the squash should be deep colored with a nonshiny finish.

store: You don't have to refrigerate winter squash; keep it in a paper bag in a cool, dark place (about 50°) for about a month. Don't store winter squash in plastic bags for more than 3 days, because the plastic traps moisture and causes the squash to rot.

prepare: Winter squash are almost impossible to overcook. They can be boiled, baked, roasted, simmered, steamed, microwaved, or sautéed.

cook: To microwave a whole squash, pierce the rind in several places so it won't explode.

chives

select: Chives should be fresh looking, crisp, and brightly-colored. Avoid herbs that have dry patches, are wilted, or look slimy.

store: Store fresh chives in a plastic bag in the refrigerator up to a week.

prepare: Fresh chives can be snipped with kitchen sheers to the desired length.

cook: Chives add a mild onion or garlic flavor and are used in cooked dishes and cold salads.

parsley

select: Fresh and dried parsley is widely available; fresh is sold in bunches in the produce department. Look for crisp, brightly colored parsley, avoiding any wilted or slimy leaves.

store: Wash parsley and shake off excess moisture. Wrap in damp paper towels; chill in a plastic bag up to a week.

prepare: If parsley begins to wilt, snip the lower stems and place the bunch in a glass of cold water; loosely cover leaves with a plastic bag, and chill. It will perk up in no time.

cook: Italian flat-leaf parsley offers a fresh flavor to stews, bean dishes, and salads.

Thyme

select: Thyme leaves should look fresh and crisp and be a vibrant green-gray in color.

store: Keep fresh thyme in a plastic bag lined with a damp paper towel in the refrigerator for up to a week.

prepare: Thyme leaves are small and often don't require chopping. Strip the leaves from their stems just before using.

cook: Thyme's earthiness is welcome with pork, lamb, duck, or goose, and it's much beloved in Cajun and Creole cooking. It's also the primary component of Caribbean jerk seasonings.

farmers market finds

local markets

Gather your family for a leisurely stroll through a local farmers market. In this community environment, you can savor the rich bounty of freshly picked fruits, vegetables, and herbs. Here we offer a partial listing of some of the South's larger farmers markets. Use it as a starting point for creating your own list of favorite markets.

Alabama

Visit www.fma.state.al.us for statewide farmers market information

Birmingham

Alabama Farmers Market:
Visit www.alabamafarmersmarket.org or call (205) 251-8737

Mt. Laurel Farmers Market:
Call (205) 408-8696

Pepper Place Market:
Visit www.pepperplacemarket.com

Clanton

Durbin Farms Market:
Call (205) 755-1672

Montgomery

State Farmers Market:
Visit www.agi.alabama.gov/farmers_market or call (334) 242-5350

Arkansas

Visit www.arkansasgrown.org for statewide farmers market information

Carlisle

Carlisle Farmers Market:
Call (870) 552-7661

Eureka Springs

Eureka Springs Farmers Market:
Contact heatherequinney@yahoo.com

North Little Rock

Central Arkansas Farmers Market:
Call (501) 231-0094

Ozark

Franklin County Farmers Market:
Call (479) 667-2525

Texarkana

Farmers' Market of Texarkana:
Call (870) 772-4558

Delaware

Visit www.farmersmarketonline.com for statewide farmers market information

Bethany

Bethany Beach Farmers Market:
Visit www.bbfm.us

Dover

Delaware State University Farmers Market: Call (302) 857-6055

Lewes

Historic Lewes Farmers Market:
Visit www.historiclewesfarmersmarket.org or call (302) 644-1436

Milford

Downtown Milford Farmers Market:
Call (302) 839-1180

New Castle Farmers Market:
Call (302) 328-4102

Wilmington

Wilmington Farmers Market at Rodney Square:
Visit www.downtownvisions.org/farmers-market or call (302) 425-5373

Florida

Visit www.florida-agriculture.com for statewide farmers market information

Flagler Beach

Flagler Beach Farmers Market:
Visit www.flaglerbeachfarmersmarket.com or call (386) 439-2881

Gainesville

Alachua County Farmers Market:
Visit www.441market.com or call (352) 371-8236

Hollywood Beach

Josh's Organic Garden:
Call (954) 456-3276

Jacksonville

Jacksonville Farmers Market:
Visit www.jaxfarmersmarket.com

Miami

Bayfront Park's Farmers Market:
Visit www.bayfrontparkmiami.com or call (305) 358-7550

Sarasota

Downtown Farmers Market:
Visit www.sarasotadowntown.com/farmers_market.html or call (941) 951-2656

Seaside

Saturday's Farmers Market:
Call (303) 819-6725

Winter Park

Winter Park Farmers Market:
Call (407) 599-3358

Ybor City

Ybor City Saturday Market:
Call (813) 241-2442

Georgia

Visit www.georgiaorganics.org for information about sustainable, locally grown food

Athens

Athens Farmers Market:
Visit www.athensfarmersmarket.net

Atlanta

Green Market for Piedmont Park:
Visit www.piedmontpark.org
or call (404) 876-4024

Morningside Farmers Market:
Visit www.morningsidemarket.com
or call (404) 313-5784

Atlanta State Farmers Market:
Call (404) 675-1782

Canton

Canton Art & Farmers Market:
Visit www.vpsgallery.com
or call 770-720-4253

Columbus

Columbus State Farmers Market:
Visit www.internationalmarketplace.us
or call (706) 332-6378

Dunwoody

**Dunwoody Spruill Green Market
(formerly known as the Spruill
Green Market):** Call (770) 214-8531

Rabun Gap

Osage Farms:
Call (706) 746-7262

Savannah

Savannah State Farmers Market:
Call (912) 966-7801

Kentucky

Visit www.kyagr.com/marketing/
farmmarket/directory.htm for statewide
farmers market information

Bowling Green

**Southern Kentucky Regional Farmers
Market:** Visit www.skyfarmersmarket.com

Lexington

Lexington Farmers Market:
Visit www.lexingtonfarmersmarket.com
or call (859) 608-2655

Louisiana

Visit www.farmersmarketonline.com for
statewide farmers market information

Baton Rouge

Red Stick Farmers Market:
Visit www.redstickfarmersmarket.org

Covington

Covington Farmers Market:
Call (985) 966-1786

New Orleans

Crescent City Farmers Market:
Visit www.crescentcityfarmersmarket.org
or call (504) 861-5898

Shreveport

**Downtown Shreveport Farmers
Market:** Call (318) 424-4000

Westwego

**Westwego Farmers & Fisheries
Market:** Visit www.cityofwestwego.com
or call (504) 341-3424

Maryland

Visit www.mda.state.md.us/md_products/
farmers_market_dir.php for statewide
farmers market information

Baltimore

Baltimore Farmers Market:
Call (410) 752-8632

Lexington Market:
Visit www.lexingtonmarket.com
or call (410) 685-6169

Bel Air

Twilight Farmers Market:
Call (410) 838-6181 ext. 114

Charlotte Hall

Charlotte Hall Farmers Market:
Call (301) 475-4200 ext. 1402

Frederick

The Great Frederick Farmers Market:
Call (301) 663-5895

Hagerstown

City Farmers Market:
Visit www.hagerstownmd.org/CityFarmers
Market/CityFarmersMarket_index.asp
or call (301) 739-8577 ext. 190

Ocean City

Ocean City Farmers Market:
Call (410) 860-2607.

Mississippi

Visit www.farmersmarketonline.com/fm/
Mississippi for statewide farmers market
information

Biloxi

Charles R. Hegwood Farmers Market:
Call (228) 435-6281

Columbus

Columbus Lowndes Farmers Market:
Call (662) 328-4164

Jackson

The Greater Belhaven Market:
Visit www.greaterbelhaven.com
or call (601) 352-8850

Tupelo

Tupelo Farmers Market:
Visit www.tupelomainstreet.com/farmers
market.html or call (662) 841-6598

Missouri

Visit www.agebb.missouri.edu/fmktdir/ for statewide farmers market information

Clayton

Clayton Farmers Market: Visit www.claytonfarmersmarket.com or call (314) 398-9729

Kansas City

KC Organics & Natural Farmers Market: Visit www.kcorganics.com or call (816) 444-3663

St. Louis

Soulard Farmers Market: Visit www.stlouis.missouri.org/citygov/soulardmarket or call (314) 622-4180

Springfield

Greater Springfield Farmers Market: Visit www.springfieldfarmersmarket.com or call (417) 833-0583

North Carolina

Visit www.ncfarmfresh.com for a directory of pick-your-own farms, roadside farm markets, and farmers markets statewide

Asheville

Western North Carolina Farmers Market: Visit www.agr.state.nc.us/markets/facilities/markets/asheville/index.htm or call (828) 253-1691

Boone

Watauga County Farmers Market: Visit www.wataugacountyfarmersmarket.org

Charlotte

Charlotte Regional Farmers Market: Visit www.ncagr.com/markets/facilities/markets/charlotte/index.htm or call (704) 357-1269

Center City Green Market: Visit www.centercitygreenmarket.com

Greensboro

Farmers Curb Market: Visit www.greensboro-nc.gov/departments/Parks/facilities/market or call (336) 373-2402

Raleigh

State Farmers Market: Visit www.ncdamarkets.org or call (919) 733-7417

Winston-Salem

Downtown Farmers Market: Visit www.dwsp.org/places_to_go/farmers_market.php or call (336) 354-1500

Dixie Classic Fairgrounds Farmers Market: Visit www.dcfair.com or call (336) 727-2236

Oklahoma

Visit www.farmersmarketonline.com for statewide farmers market information

Bethany

The Children's Center Farmers Market: Visit www.tccokc.org or call (405) 470-2259

Oklahoma City

Oklahoma State University-Oklahoma City Farmers' Market: Visit www.osuokc.edu/farmersmarket or call (405) 947-4421

Tulsa

Cherry Street Farmers' Market: Visit www.cherrystreetfarmersmarket.com or call (918) 519-9383

South Carolina

Visit www.farmersmarketonline.com for statewide farmers market information

Charleston

Charleston Farmers Market: Call (843) 724-7309

Mount Pleasant Farmers Market:

Visit www.townofmountpleasant.com or call (843) 884-8517

Columbia

Columbia State Farmers Market: Visit www.scda.state.sc.us

Florence

Pee Dee State Farmers Market: Visit www.pdfarmersmarket.sc.gov or call (843) 665-5154

Greenville

Greenville State Farmers Market: Visit www.scda.state.sc.us

Ridgeland

Jasper County Farmers Market: Visit www.jaspercountysc.org or call (843) 726-8127

Tennessee

Visit www.farmersmarketonline.com for statewide farmers market information

Chattanooga

The Chattanooga Market: Visit www.chattanoogamarket.com

Knoxville

Market Square Farmers Market: Visit www.knoxvillemarketsquare.com or call (865) 405-3135

Memphis

Agricenter International Farmers Market Visit www.agricenter.org or call (901) 355-1977

Memphis Farmers Market: Visit www.memphisfarmersmarket.org or call (901) 575-0592

Nashville

Nashville Farmers Market: Visit www.nashvillefarmersmarket.org or call (615) 880-2001

Texas

Visit www.farmersmarketonline.com for statewide farmers market information

Austin

Austin Farmers Market:
Visit www.austinfarmersmarket.org or call (512) 236-0074 ext.101

Brownsville

The Brownsville Farmers Market:
Visit www.brownsvillefarmersmarket.org or call (956) 882-5895

Coppell

Coppell Farmers Market:
Visit www.coppellfarmersmarket.org or call (972) 304-7043

Dallas

Dallas Farmers Market:
Visit www.dallasfarmersmarket.org or call (214) 939-2808

Galveston

Galveston Farmers Market:
Visit www.downtowngalveston.org/about_the_market.html or call (409) 763-7080

Grand Prairie

Grand Prairie Farmers Market:
Call (972) 237-8036

Houston

Bayou City Farmers' Market:
Visit www.urbanharvest.org or call (713) 880-5540

Lubbock

Lubbock Farmers' Market:
Visit www.vintagetownship.com or call (806) 771-1117

Marfa

Farm Stand Marfa:
Call (917) 215-6933

Virginia

Visit www.farmersmarketonline.com for statewide farmers market information

Charlottesville

Charlottesville City Market:
Visit www.charlottesvillecitymarket.com or call (434) 970-3371

Chesapeake

Edinburgh Green Market:
Visit www.edinburghcommons.net or call (757) 497-7700

Leesburg

Leesburg Farmers Market:
Visit www.LoudounFarms.org

Middleburg

Middleburg Farmers Market:
Visit www.middleburg.org

The Plains

Archwood Green Barns Farmers Market: Call (540) 253-5289

Richmond

17th Street Farmers Market:
Visit www.17thstreetfarmersmarket.com or call (804) 646-0477

Roanoke

Historic Roanoke City Market:
Visit www.downtownroanoke.org or call (540) 342-2028.

Virginia Beach

City of Virginia Beach Farmers Market: Visit www.vbgov.com/farmersmarket or call (757) 385-4395

Old Beach Farmers Market:
Visit www.oldbeachfarmersmarket.com or call (757) 428-5444

Red Mill Green Market:
Visit www.redmillcommons.net or call (757) 497-7700

Williamsburg

Williamsburg Farmers Market:
Visit www.williamsburgfarmersmarket.com or call (757) 259-3768

Washington, D.C.

Visit www.dc.about.com/od/restaurants/a/FarmersMktsDC.htm for farmers market information in Washington, D.C.

Dupont Circle FRESHFARM Market:
Visit www.freshfarmmarket.org or call (202) 362-8889

Eastern Market:
Visit www.easternmarketdc.com

Foggy Bottom FRESHFARM Market:
Visit www.freshfarmmarket.org or call (202) 362-8889

Penn Quarter FRESHFARM Market:
Visit www.freshfarmmarket.org or call (202) 362-8889

West Virginia

Visit www.wvu.edu/~agexten/farmman2/farmmrkts for statewide farmers market information

Charleston

Capitol Market:
Visit www.capitolmarket.net or call (304) 344-1905

Huntington

Cabell County Tailgate Farmers Market: Visit www.centralcitymarket.com or call (304) 525-1500

Morgantown

Morgantown Farmers Market:
Visit www.morgantownfarmers.org or call (304) 291-7201

food festivals

Great food crafts, music, and fun await the whole family at these festivals. Dates, times, locations, and Web addresses of markets and festivals were current at the time of publication but are subject to change. To confirm current information, please call market/festival contacts ahead of time, or visit their Web sites before planning a visit.

Alabama

Baldwin County Strawberry Festival — April Loxley, AL; Visit www.baldwincountystrawberryfestival.org

Alabama Blueberry Festival — June Brewton, AL; Visit www.alabamablueberryfestival.com

Alabama Butterbean Festival — September Pinson, AL; Call (205) 390-1952

National Peanut Festival — October Dothan, AL; Visit www.nationalpeanutfestival.com

Arkansas

Alma Spinach Festival — April Alma, AR; Visit www.almaspinachfestival.com

Crawfish Festival — May Dermott, AR; Visit www.dermottcrawfishfestival.com

Bradley County Pink Tomato Festival — June Warren, AR; Visit www.bradleypinktomato.com

Annual Johnson County Peach Festival — June Clarksville, AR; Visit www.jocopeachfestival.8m.com

Florida

Annual Kumquat Festival — January Dade City, FL; Visit www.kumquatfestival.org

Newberry Watermelon Festival — May Newberry, FL; Visit www.newberrywatermelonfestival.com

Annual International Mango Festival — July Coral Gables, FL; Visit www.fairchildgarden.org

Georgia

Vidalia Onion Festival — April Vidalia, GA; Visit www.vidaliaonionfestival.com

Farm Day — September Lumber City, GA; Call (912) 363-2133

Shrimp & Grits Festival — September Jekyll Island, GA; Call (912) 635-4189

Plains Peanut Festival — September Plains, GA; Call (229) 824-5373

Taste of Atlanta — October Atlanta, GA; Call (404) 875-4434

Kentucky

Spoonbread Festival — September Berea, KY; Call (859) 986-9760

Louisiana

Ponchatoula Strawberry Festival — April Ponochatoula, LA; Visit www.lastrawberryfestival.com

New Orleans Wine & Food Experience — May New Orleans, LA; Visit www.nowfe.com

Louisiana Watermelon Festival — July Farmerville, LA; Visit www.lawatermelonfestival.com

Louisiana Yambilee Festival — October Opelousas, LA; Visit www.yambilee.com

La Cuisine de Beauregard — November DeRidder, LA; Call (337) 462-8900

Maryland

St. Michaels Food & Wine Festival — April St. Michaels, MD; Visit www.stmichaelsfoodandwinefestival.com

Autumn Wine Festival — October Salisbury, MD; Visit www.autumnwinefestival.org

Mississippi

Natchez Food & Wine Festival — July/August Natchez, MS; Visit www.natchezfoodfest.com

Missouri

Mushroom Festival — May Richmond, MO; Visit www.richmondchamber.org/festival

Annual Great Stone Hill Grape Stomp — August Hermann, MO; Visit www.stonehillwinery.com

North Carolina

North Carolina Pickle Festival — April Mount Olive, NC; Visit www.ncpicklefest.org

North Carolina Blueberry Festival — June Burgaw, NC; Visit www.ncblueberryfestival.com

Apple Fest — September Winston Salem, NC; Call (336) 924-8191

Farmers Festival — October Fairmont, NC; Call (910) 628-9766

Apple Harvest Festival — October
Waynesville, NC; Call (828) 456-3021

Black Walnut Festival — October
Bethania, NC; Call (336) 922-0434

Oklahoma

Ponca City Herb Festival — June
Ponca City, OK; Visit www.poncacity
herbfestival.net

South Carolina

Taste of Charleston — October
Charleston, SC; Visit www.charleston
restaurantassociation.com

Collard Festival — November
Gaston, SC; Call (803) 796-7725

Tennessee

**West Tennessee Strawberry
Festival — May** Humboldt, TN;
Visit www.wtsf.org

**Annual Taste of Loudon
County — October** Lenoir City, TN;
Visit www.visitloudoncounty.com/
events.php

Texas

Annual Savor Dallas — March
Dallas, TX; Visit www.savordallas.com

Poteet Strawberry Festival — April
Poteet, TX; Visit www.strawberry
festival.com

**Annual Texas Blueberry
Festival — June** Nacogdoches, TX;
Visit www.texasblueberryfestival.com

Annual Pecan Festival — September
Mansfield, TX; Visit www.mansfield
chamber.org/PecanFestival.asp

**East Texas Arboretum Fall
Festival — October** Athens, TX;
Call (903) 675-5630

Texas Mushroom Festival — October
Madisonville, TX; Call (936) 348-3592

Peanut Festival — October
Whitesboro, TX; Call (903) 564-3331

Virginia

Highland Maple Festival — March
Monterey, VA; Visit www.highlandcounty.
org/maple.htm

**Maymont Herbs Galore &
More — April** Maymont, VA;
Visit www.maymont.org

**Chincoteague Island Bluberry
Festival — July** Chincoteague Island,
VA; Visit www.chincoteagueblueberry
festival.com

**Annual Boones Mill Apple
Festival — September** Boones Mill, VA;
Visit www.boonesmillapplefestival.com

**Annual Virginia Peanut
Festival — September** Emporia, VA;
Visit www.thevirginiapeanutfestival.com

**Charlottesville Vegetarian
Festival — September** Charlottesville,
VA; Visit www.cvillevegfest.org

Washington, D.C.

**Washington D.C. International Wine &
Food Festival — February** Washington,
D.C.; Visit www.wine-expos.com/wine/dc

West Virginia

**West Virginia Black Walnut
Festival — October** Spencer, WV;
Visit www.wvblackwalnutfestival.org

resources on the web

Check out these online resources for more information on farmers markets and local farmers.

www.southernliving.com

www.ams.usda.gov/farmersmarkets

www.fruitstands.com

www.farmersmarket.com

www.localharvest.org

www.gardeners.com

www.seedsofchange.com

www.communitygarden.org

www.pickyourown.org

www.locallygrown.net

www.eatwellguide.org

metric equivalents

The recipes that appear in this cookbook use the standard U.S. method for measuring liquid and dry or solid ingredients (teaspoons, tablespoons, and cups). The information in the following charts is provided to help cooks outside the United States successfully use these recipes. All equivalents are approximate.

Metric Equivalents for Different Types of Ingredients

A standard cup measure of a dry or solid ingredient will vary in weight depending on the type of ingredient. A standard cup of liquid is the same volume for any type of liquid. Use the following chart when converting standard cup measures to grams (weight) or milliliters (volume).

Standard Cup	Fine Powder (ex. flour)	Grain (ex. rice)	Granular (ex. sugar)	Liquid Solids (ex. butter)	Liquid (ex. milk)
1	140 g	150 g	190 g	200 g	240 ml
¾	105 g	113 g	143 g	150 g	180 ml
⅔	93 g	100 g	125 g	133 g	160 ml
½	70 g	75 g	95 g	100 g	120 ml
⅓	47 g	50 g	63 g	67 g	80 ml
¼	35 g	38 g	48 g	50 g	60 ml
⅛	18 g	19 g	24 g	25 g	30 ml

Useful Equivalents for Dry Ingredients by Weight

(To convert ounces to grams, multiply the number of ounces by 30.)

1 oz	=	$\frac{1}{16}$ lb	=	30 g
4 oz	=	¼ lb	=	120 g
8 oz	=	½ lb	=	240 g
12 oz	=	¾ lb	=	360 g
16 oz	=	1 lb	=	480 g

Useful Equivalents for Length

(To convert inches to centimeters, multiply the number of inches by 2.5.)

1 in				=	2.5 cm			
6 in	=	½ ft		=	15 cm			
12 in	=	1 ft		=	30 cm			
36 in	=	3 ft	=	1 yd	=	90 cm		
40 in				=	100 cm	=	1 m	

Useful Equivalents for Liquid Ingredients by Volume

¼ tsp					=	1 ml	
½ tsp					=	2 ml	
1 tsp					=	5 ml	
3 tsp	=	1 Tbsp		½ fl oz	=	15 ml	
		2 Tbsp	=	⅛ cup	=	1 fl oz	=	30 ml
		4 Tbsp	=	¼ cup	=	2 fl oz	=	60 ml
		5⅓ Tbsp	=	⅓ cup	=	3 fl oz	=	80 ml
		8 Tbsp	=	½ cup	=	4 fl oz	=	120 ml
		10⅔ Tbsp	=	⅔ cup	=	5 fl oz	=	160 ml
		12 Tbsp	=	¾ cup	=	6 fl oz	=	180 ml
		16 Tbsp	=	1 cup	=	8 fl oz	=	240 ml
		1 pt	=	2 cups	=	16 fl oz	=	480 ml
		1 qt	=	4 cups	=	32 fl oz	=	960 ml
					33 fl oz	=	1000 ml = 1 l

Useful Equivalents for Cooking/Oven Temperatures

	Fahrenheit	Celsius	Gas Mark
Freeze water	32° F	0° C	
Room temperature	68° F	20° C	
Boil water	212° F	100° C	
Bake	325° F	160° C	3
	350° F	180° C	4
	375° F	190° C	5
	400° F	200° C	6
	425° F	220° C	7
	450° F	230° C	8
Broil			Grill

index